D0538424

Mrs. O

The Face of Fashion Democracy

MARY TOMER

DESIGNED BY

RODRIGO CORRAL DESIGN

NEW YORK · BOSTON · NASHVILLE

Center Street
Hachette Book Group
237 Park Avenue
New York, NY 10017

Visit our Web site at www.centerstreet.com.

Center Street is a division of
Hachette Book Group, Inc.
The Center Street name and logo are trademarks
of Hachette Book Group, Inc.

Designed by Rodrigo Corral Design

Printed in Singapore

First Edition: November 2009
10 9 8 7 6 5 4 3 2 1

ISBN 978-1-59995-258-1
LCCN: 2009931154

This book is dedicated to Michelle Obama,
first lady of the United States—
the woman who unites and inspires us all.

CONTENTS

INTRODUCTION

Perched on my couch in August 2008, I intently watched the Democratic National Convention coverage. I had already tuned into Michelle Obama's style as media stories began to surface every few months—a profile in *Vogue*, a feature story in the *New York Times*, and who could have missed the frenzy sparked by the black and white Donna Ricco dress worn on *The View*? But it was during the convention that I became captivated.

I found myself profoundly impressed by Michelle Obama's confidence, intelligence, and gracious spirit, and inspired that such strength and self possession could exist in harmony with a feminine, almost romantic, style sensibility. While strong and feminine shouldn't be at odds, the dress codes of our culture can be remarkably outdated, particularly in the realm of politics. With Mrs. Obama's style, a new era of body-hugging silhouettes, jewel tones, floral prints, and brooches was ushered in—unapologetically feminine details that quickly dismissed the boxy skirt suit as anonymous, old-fashioned, and, well, square.

On a more immediate level, I was simply taken with her beautiful clothes. By the second night of the convention, I was excitedly Googling to find out more. Who had designed her dress? Was the fabric a brocade? And what did others think?

Certainly, I couldn't be the only one interested. Unable to find a central online resource that tracked and discussed Michelle Obama's style, I decided to create my own blog and sought help from my employer to build and design it—the genesis of Mrs-O.org. The site has grown into a buzzing community, attracting women and men of all ages, from all parts of the world. Its success has, in turn, led to the wonderful opportunity of writing this book.

It is difficult for many, myself included, to separate how we feel about Michelle Obama, the woman, and how we feel about her style. We are intrigued by the composite woman—an accomplished professional; a devoted mother, wife, and daughter; a woman in touch with her own well-being, who manages to pull it all off with an impeccably chic sense of style. We can perceive that the same qualities we admire in the first lady—her energetic spirit, intelligence and authenticity—also radiate through her clothes.

At their most basic, clothes are a form of creative expression and visual communication. And in the way that clothes can speak without using words, Michelle Obama's style speaks volumes. Through her clothes, Mrs. Obama conveys astute awareness of the occasion and mood, choosing ensembles that are full of nuanced meaning: collegiate to meet school children, modern professional to tour federal agencies, understated elegance to meet the Queen of England, knock-out glamour to host a state dinner.

While the first lady's wardrobe has become regular fodder for the global media, a story not as widely told is the substance of the clothes themselves. Mrs. Obama's wardrobe is largely acquired through Chicago's Ikram, one of the most progressive and fashion-forward boutiques in the world. Its owner and curator, Ikram Goldman, has taken on an unofficial role as advisor and style confidante for the first lady. It is Ikram's masterful, unerring eye, in great part, that has presented the first lady with such a range of wonderful designers to choose from. Their designs compose a wardrobe increasingly known for its diversity and eclecticism— qualities that reflect the way a modern, twenty-first century woman dresses.

At the high end of fashion, Mrs. Obama has gravitated toward designers who value old-world craftsmanship and independent thinking. She has eschewed many of the "big names" in favor of smaller, well-established ateliers and rising design stars. Through Michelle Obama's patronage, American designers have received national and international recognition, many for the first time. While Mrs. Obama has done wonders to bolster the American fashion industry, she has embraced select European and Japanese designers as well.

Mrs. Obama's style is not limited to high design. She incorporates the full spectrum of fashion, as designs from affordable retailers are seamlessly mixed into her wardrobe. For the first time in history, Americans have access to the very same clothes the first lady wears, a gesture that conveys a down-to-earth sensibility. But the magic lies in the balance. Mrs. Obama's style adeptly unites accessibility with high wattage glamour. We relate to the clothes—like the woman—as both familiar and inspirational.

Democracy exists not just in the fashion, but in the perspective. Mrs-O.org has become an authority on Michelle Obama's style, a forum for people to share different points of view and mutual enthusiasm about the first lady's style. This book contains commentary from those inside the fashion community, who know the ins and outs of the industry best, and ends with final words from the site community—real world style experts in their own right.

Michelle Obama's personal style has become remarkable common ground, connecting us in a real and human way, even in the blogosphere. My intent with this book is to capture the inspiration that the first lady—and her impeccable, democratic sense of style—offers to so many of us.

CHAPTER I THE EARLY YEARS

First Sketches

JANUARY 17, 1964

Michelle LaVaughn Robinson is born in Chicago. She and her brother Craig, two years older, are raised by their parents Fraser and Marian Robinson. They live on the top floor of a brick bungalow on the South Side of the city. Michelle's great-aunt, who lives downstairs, teaches Michelle to play the piano. Michelle's mother, Marian Robinson, would later tell *Chicago* magazine, "she would practice the piano for so long you'd have to tell her to stop."

1970s

Michelle skips the second grade, and by the sixth grade, joins a gifted class at Bryn Mawr Elementary (now the Bouchet Math and Science Academy). She would describe her childhood to *The New Yorker*, "Not a whole lot of money. Going to the circus once a year was a big deal. Getting pizza on Friday was a treat. Summers were long and fun."

1981

Michelle Robinson graduates from Whitney Young High School, Chicago's first magnet high school. She is on the honor roll all four years, a member of the National Honor Society, and graduates as class salutatorian.

Michelle follows her older brother Craig to the east coast to attend Princeton. Two classes ahead of his sister, he would become the university's star basketball player. She would later recall adjusting to life at Princeton in *Vogue*: "I remember being shocked by college students who drove BMWs. I didn't even know parents who drove BMWs."

847
848
849
850
856
858
859
860

1985

Michelle graduates cum laude with a bachelor of arts from Princeton University, where she majors in sociology and minors in African American studies.

1988

Michelle Robinson graduates with her J.D. from Harvard Law School. At Harvard, she would work at the Legal Aid Bureau, representing clients who couldn't afford lawyers.

Michelle returns to Chicago to accept a position with the corporate law firm Sidley Austin; she works as an associate in the marketing and intellectual-property group.

SUMMER 1989

Michelle meets Barack Obama, a first-year intern at Sidley Austin. Michelle is assigned to be his advisor. Despite hesitation on her part because of their professional relationship, the two begin dating. For their first official date, Barack takes Michelle to the Art Institute of Chicago, to lunch at the museum's outdoor café, and later to see Spike Lee's *Do the Right Thing*. According to the *Chicago Sun-Times*, Michelle has said of the date, "He was definitely putting on the charm. . . . He swept me off my feet."

1991

Michelle Robinson's father, Fraser, passes away at the age of 56.

Barack proposes to Michelle at Gordon's on Clark Street. Dessert is served with an engagement ring on the side.

JULY 1991

Michelle leaves Sidley Austin to work for Chicago Mayor Richard M. Daley's office. She take a position as assistant to the Chicago mayor, specializing in human service initiatives. Michelle later told *The Daily Princetonian* of her decision to leave the private sector: "[Barack and I] had many debates about how to best effect change," she said. "We both wanted to affect the community on a larger scale than either of us could individually, and we wanted to do it outside of big corporations."

1992

Michelle is named the assistant commissioner in the city of Chicago's Department of Planning and Development.

OCTOBER 18, 1992

Barack and Michelle Obama are married at Trinity United Church of Christ. Santita Jackson, daughter of Rev. Jesse Jackson Sr., sings at the wedding.

1993

Michelle Obama becomes Executive Director for Chicago office of Public Allies, a non-profit organization for young adults pursuing careers in public service. She works there for nearly four years, establishing an office, board of directors, and significant funding.

1996

Michelle Obama is named the Associate Dean of Student Services at the University of Chicago, where she develops the University's Community Service Center.

Barack Obama is elected to the Illinois Senate, where he will continue to serve through 2004.

JULY 1998

Michelle gives birth to Malia Ann Obama.

NOVEMBER 7, 2000

Barack Obama has an unsuccessful bid for a seat in the U.S. House of Representatives.

JUNE 2001

Michelle gives birth to Natasha (known as "Sasha") Obama.

2002

Michelle Obama is named Executive Director for Community Affairs for the University of Chicago Hospitals. She serves as a liaison between the hospital and surrounding community.

JULY 2004

Barack Obama, United States Senate candidate for Illinois, delivers a keynote address at Democratic National Convention in Boston.

OCTOBER 2004

Michelle Obama is profiled in *Chicago* magazine; the feature is titled, "First Lady in Waiting."

NOVEMBER 2, 2004

Barack Obama is elected as the junior United States senator from Illinois.

JANUARY 4, 2005

Barack Obama is sworn in as the United States senator from Illinois at the state capitol in Springfield, Illinois.

MAY 2005

Michelle Obama is promoted to the Vice President for Community and External Affairs for the University of Chicago Hospitals. Through her job, she encourages low-income South Side residents to use community-based health clinics rather than more expensive, less efficient emergency rooms.

AUGUST 2006

Michelle and Barack Obama travel to Africa, where Barack Obama visits his father's birthplace in rural western Kenya.

FEBRUARY 10, 2007

Barack Obama announces his run for president of the United States in Springfield, Illinois.

CHAPTER II PRIMARY CAMPAIGN

Dressed for Change

With the launch of her husband's presidential campaign, Michelle Obama began to move into the national spotlight. While she was comfortable with public speaking, thanks to her job at the University of Chicago Medical Center as Vice President for Community and External Affairs, she had not played a prominent role in her husband's past campaigns.

Yet almost immediately, her charm and ability to connect with people proved to be a valuable asset to the campaign. Barack Obama began to call her "The Closer" for her ability to resonate with voters.

For her expanded duties on the political stage, Mrs. Obama turned repeatedly to the two Chicago women who sartorially knew her best: designer Maria Pinto and boutique owner Ikram Goldman. "Some people were amazed that there were great fashion choices in Chicago," says Timothy Long, costume and textile curator for the Chicago History Museum. "But those people don't know their history. For decades, glamorous women here have been using dress to prove that there is a high level of sophistication in Chicago."

During the primary campaign, Mrs. Obama wore a predominance of Maria Pinto designs. When named to *Vanity Fair's* Best-Dressed List for 2007, Mrs. Obama cited Pinto as her favorite designer.

While Maria Pinto made her name first by designing luxurious wraps and evening wear, she had expanded her daytime line significantly. "I love creating these make-an-entrance evening dresses," Maria Pinto told *Chicago* magazine. "But we all have daytime lives. Women need clothes that work but also look wonderful." Mrs. Obama's choices helped showcase Pinto's new direction, which married a sophisticated feminine style with slightly edgy, flirtatious appeal.

Fitted sheath dresses, many designed by Maria Pinto, became a signature of Mrs. Obama's style during this time period. "Mrs. Obama's clothing choices are diverse, but she seems to favor the shift dress, which is ideal for her body type," said Andrew Bolton, curator, The Costume Institute, The Metropolitan Museum of Art. "It expresses her youthfulness and athleticism, two of the traits that, traditionally, have symbolized the 'American Woman.'"

Michelle Obama wears a wool crepe dress by Maria Pinto. She waits backstage at the North Carolina State University arena in Raleigh, North Carolina, May 6, 2008.

SATURDAY, FEBRUARY 10, 2007

ON A SINGLE-DIGIT FRIGID MORNING, the launch of the Obama presidential campaign started outdoors, in front of the Old State Capitol building in Springfield, Illinois. The location was weighted with history, for it was here that Abraham Lincoln spent important early years in his political career.

Running For President

In spite of daunting weather, thousands of people crowded into the town square to witness the historic speech and to welcome the Obama family to the presidential race. Mrs. Obama braved the chill in a black coat made of alpaca. The coat, designed by Maria Pinto, was light in weight yet comfortably warm. It sported a large portrait collar, which drew attention to Mrs. Obama's face, accented by a purple cashmere scarf. Bracelet-length gloves and a small-brimmed hat in black complemented her winter wrap, while cuffed, wide-leg wool pants and high-heeled black boots finished the look.

Maria Pinto fashioned this coat specifically for this memorable occasion, with an eye on comfort and a streamlined, almost graphic silhouette that would photograph well. While discussing the details of this design, Pinto asked about what coats the Obama daughters would be wearing. Mrs. Obama answered that she had not had time to shop for them yet. Pinto offered to make coats for the girls, too.

For Malia, Pinto made a black wool coat with fullness similar to the coat Mrs. Obama wore; it was accessorized with white knit gloves, scarf, and cap; for Sasha, Pinto chose a black-and-white houndstooth check, with hot pink knit accessories. Senator Obama wore his classic charcoal black overcoat and scarf. The final result was a picture perfect tableau of a young American family, coordinated but still individuals. Standing together on the steps of the Old State Capitol, waving to the crowds, their message was clear: We are in this together.

It was an evocative way to face down the wind chill, as well as the long and winding campaign road ahead—not to mention a stylish beginning to the official campaign.

> "Her style is timeless. She possesses a natural sophistication. But what I love most is her brilliance and eloquence coupled by the grace and beauty of a dancer."
>
> **MARIA PINTO**

Perry, IA

THE POLITICAL STRATEGY OF THE OBAMA CAMPAIGN centered on winning the caucuses in Iowa—the first primary vote of 2008. Both the Obamas visited the state repeatedly, getting to know the voters through small gatherings.

On a beautiful spring day, Mrs. Obama attended a neighborhood coffee in Perry, Iowa. For this backyard gathering, she chose an ensemble by Maria Pinto: a sleeveless blouse in apricot silk charmeuse paired with a pencil skirt in cotton. An oversize leather belt defined her waist. Overall, the look conveyed a ladylike accessibility—an ideal message for meeting voters.

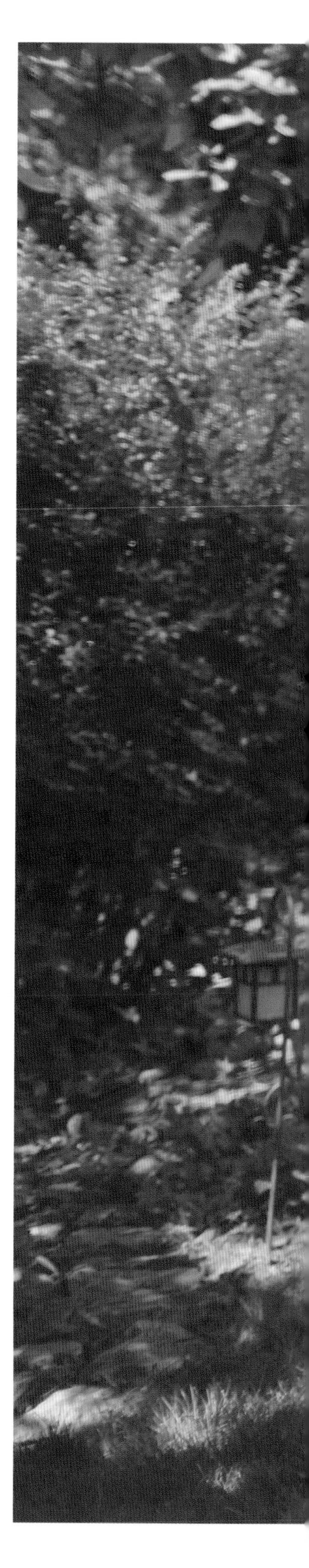

The Women's
Conference

TUESDAY, OCTOBER 23, 2007

Pictured left to right: Jeri Thompson, Cindy McCain, Michelle Obama, Ann Romney, Elizabeth Edwards, and Maria Shriver.

AT THE WOMEN'S CONFERENCE IN LONG BEACH, CALIFORNIA, Maria Shriver—wife of California Governor Arnold Schwarzenegger and accomplished television reporter—brought together presidential candidates' spouses for a roundtable discussion. Five political spouses from both the Democratic and Republican parties participated: Cindy McCain, Jeri Thompson, Ann Romney, Elizabeth Edwards, and Michelle Obama.

Mrs. Obama, who spoke of her efforts to find a balance between family and political obligations, wore a houndstooth check sheath dress by Oscar de la Renta. The dress, from the designer's Fall 2007 collection, featured an inset natural waist and hallmark de la Renta touches: texture and surface embellishment. A trim of black metallic cord and ball buttons accented the jewel collar neckline and short sleeves. It also ran in a vertical line down the front of the dress and encircled the waist. The resulting cross of trim created a geometric interest that played off the pattern of the check fabric.

Oscar de la Renta was born in the Dominican Republic; as an adult, he moved to the U.S. and became a fashion designer for Elizabeth Arden. He started his own line in 1965. Known for creating elegant clothes for an opulent world, Mr. de la Renta has long been a favorite of society women and past first ladies, including Jacqueline Kennedy, Nancy Reagan, Hillary Clinton, and Laura Bush. In 2009, the designer would criticize Michelle Obama for her fashion choices as first lady, later apologizing for his ill-chosen words. What most didn't realize was that Michelle Obama had, in fact, worn Oscar de la Renta designs in the past, notably for this October 2007 event.

SATURDAY, JANUARY 26, 2008

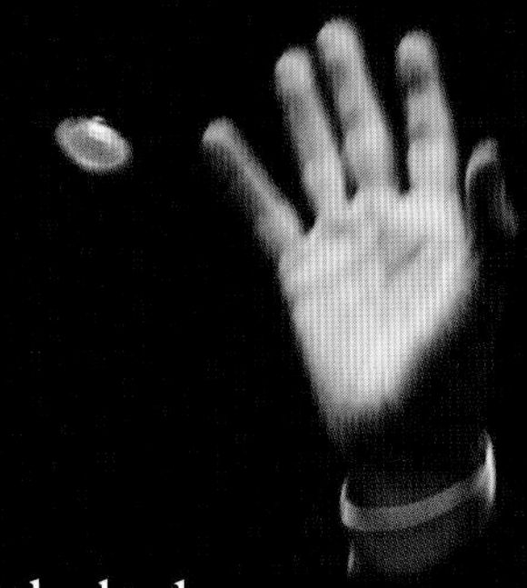

Columbia, SC

IN SOUTH CAROLINA, the primary campaign battle had at times been fiercely fought. So Barack Obama's decisive win that Saturday night helped pave his path to the White House. Former South Carolina Gov. Jim Hodges called the dramatic margin of victory "a first-round knockout."

When the Obamas took the stage for a victory celebration, they and the crowd of supporters were jubilant. "Tonight the cynics who believed that what began in the snows of Iowa was just an illusion were told a different story by the good people of South Carolina," said Senator Obama.

The Obamas appeared color coordinated, with the ruby stripes of Barack Obama's tie complementing Mrs. Obama's dark raspberry tweed suit, implicitly sending a message that they were a team. The cut of Mrs. Obama's jacket was form fitting and flirty, with its nipped-in waist and flared sleeves balanced by a matching pencil skirt. A cream blouse and a three-strand necklace of pearls completed her look.

The suit was made by Peter Soronen, a one-time Chicagoan who got his start in the fashion business by designing wedding dresses. This was the first significant public event where Mrs. Obama wore one of his creations. She had chosen the suit from the luxury Chicago boutique Ikram.

Chicago, IL

TO WATCH THE RETURNS ON SUPER TUESDAY—the day when the greatest number of states conduct primary elections—the Obamas returned to Chicago. It was a hometown crowd of supporters, including designer Maria Pinto, who greeted them at a rally held at the Hyatt Regency Chicago.

For the occasion, Mrs. Obama wore another Pinto design: a red sheath dress of four-ply silk crepe with a matching waist-length jacket. The voluminous, elbow-length bell sleeves provided a romantic, almost Renaissance note to the otherwise minimalist lines of this outfit. While the dramatic sleeves were a temporary departure from Mrs. Obama's love of clean, modern lines, certain elements of her trademark style could be discerned—notably, her choice of a figure-hugging sheath dress and bold color.

It was almost one year ago to the day that the Obamas had started the presidential campaign in Springfield, Illinois. And while the nomination was still in play, the atmosphere that night was one of a victorious homecoming. "It is good to be home," said Barack Obama. "And it's good to have Michelle home." The reprieve from the campaign trail would be short, but that night it didn't matter.

WEDNESDAY, FEBRUARY 20, 2008

Providence, RI

MICHELLE OBAMA WAS THE FEATURED SPEAKER for the launch event of the campaign group Rhode Island Women for Obama. For her appearance, she wore a dark pant suit with pinstripes by Alexander McQueen. The suit, which featured strikingly wide lapels and high-waisted pants, was part of McQueen's Spring 2008 collection. Underneath the jacket, Mrs. Obama wore a scoop neck white top. An openwork flower brooch accented her lapel, bringing a touch of feminine charm and sparkle to the tailored outfit.

Born in England, Alexander McQueen began his work in fashion through an apprenticeship to a Savile Row tailor. It was there, making bespoke men's suits, that McQueen honed his attention to fine detailing and richly defined finishing touches. After Savile Row, he worked for a theatrical costume company. He then traveled to Milan and worked for designer Romeo Gigli.

Returning to London, he attended Central Saint Martins College of Art and Design, the city's most prestigious fashion school, where he earned a master's degree. Out of school, he quickly developed a reputation as an edgy designer who loved to shock his runway audiences. His designs, too, were rebellious and extremely dramatic; they often drew extensively on his past experiences on Savile Row and in theatrical costuming.

> "She operates on tastes and instincts, and doesn't follow the crowd."
>
> **WENDY DONAHUE,** *THE CHICAGO TRIBUNE*

Not much has changed in 20 years, as the designer has built his successful namesake label. A prime example: when shown on the runway, the suit jacket worn by Michelle Obama was originally paired with coordinating hotpants. Mrs. Obama would again wear an Alexander McQueen piece—a tailored black jacket, trimmed with a scarlet ruffle—for the September 2008 cover of *Ebony*.

In Providence, Mrs. Obama spoke to the audience of the "amazing journey" the campaign was providing her. She mentioned, in particular, the chance to travel the country and listen to people who, otherwise, she would not have had the chance to meet.

CHANGE
WE CAN
BELIEVE IN

WEDNESDAY, MAY 14, 2008

San Juan, PR

WITH HER HAIR SWEPT BACK IN A CHIGNON, Michelle Obama stepped off the plane in San Juan, Puerto Rico, dressed for both the occasion and the temperature. Once again, she chose fashions by Maria Pinto. Both her Rachel blouse and Talia skirt were made of cotton—the blouse in soft white and blue-gray stripes, and the skirt in a solid stone color.

The blouse featured a racer back design and origami-inspired ruffle at the neckline, created by small squares of material irregularly stacked and folded in a series. The simple lines of the pencil skirt helped showcase the dramatic collar of the blouse. A wide leather belt with laser cut detail completed Mrs. Obama's look.

Governor Aníbal Acevedo Vilá and his wife Luisa greeted Mrs. Obama plane-side; they would serve as her hosts for the two-day visit. On her first day in Puerto Rico, they toured the San Jorge Children's Hospital in San Juan, where Mrs. Obama spent time with young patients. The next day, they visited the Caguas Botanical Gardens, where a campaign event was held.

"We will continue to build a relationship of trust and respect, that only comes from interaction," Mrs. Obama told a crowd of supporters. "And it's with conversations, it's with shared stories, it's with hugs—it's with all that stuff that builds relationship, that has very little to do with politics and has everything to do with interacting with people."

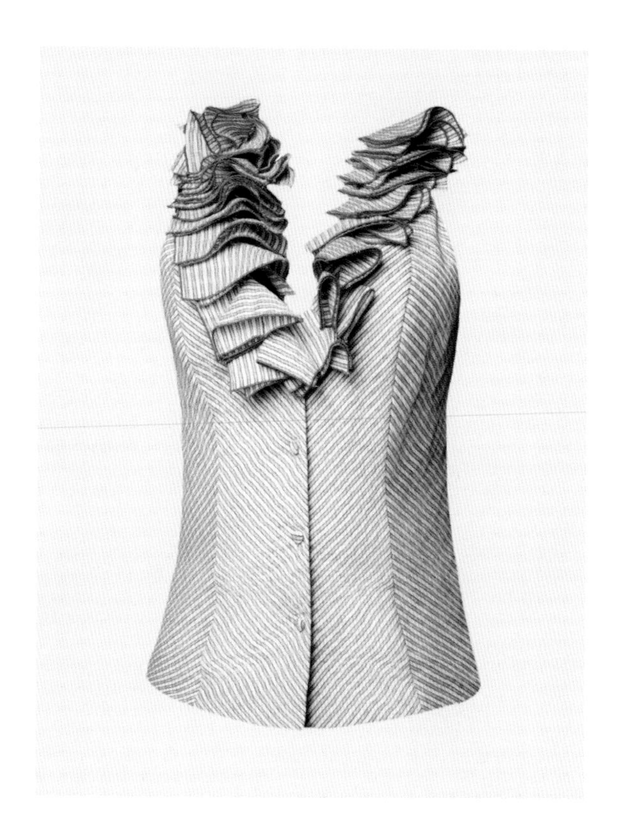

ABOVE: Maria Pinto Rachel blouse.

RIGHT: Michelle Obama meets with a young patient at San Jorge Children's Hospital in San Juan, Puerto Rico.

TUESDAY, MAY 20, 2008

Des Moines, IA

ON A BALMY SPRING NIGHT, the Obamas celebrated a primary victory in Oregon by returning to Des Moines, Iowa. "There is a spirit that brought us here tonight, a spirit of change and hope and possibility," said Senator Obama.

Mrs. Obama wore an olive green suit from Moschino's Spring 2008 collection. The jacket featured a funnel neckline, elbow-length sleeves, and hidden placket. The skirt, with two inverted pleats on the front, had a slightly belled shape. Mrs. Obama added a belt from Erickson Beamon's Techno Deco line that brought a spark of color to the ensemble, as well as a sheen that matched the suit's luminous material. In August 2008, while she toured the stage at the beginning of the Democratic Party Convention, Mrs. Obama wore the jacket again—this time unbelted—over black pants. "That chartreuse tone that Mrs. Obama often wears has now become, for my team and myself, 'Obama Green,'" Rossella Jardini, creative director for Moschino, later told *Women's Wear Daily*.

Rossella Jardini was named the creative director of Moschino in 1994, following the death of her close friend Franco Moschino, the founder of the Moschino brand. Franco Moschino achieved international success for his outstanding creativity and artistic originality. By twisting irony and elegance in all of her collections, Rossella Jardini carries on Franco Moschino's vision, reinterpreting the classics with the creativity that defines Moschino.

Olive green jacket and skirt from Moschino's Spring 2008 collection.

THE
GIFT
SHOP

Barack and Michelle Obama share a moment backstage at a campaign rally in Des Moines, Iowa.

ON THIS NIGHT, Barack Obama claimed the presidential nomination of the Democratic Party. Although the convention was more than two months away, the celebration in St. Paul, Minnesota, felt like the beginning of the convention process.

Primary Campaign Victory

For this historic evening, Michelle Obama wore a purple silk sheath dress by Maria Pinto. It was sleeveless and form-fitting, and featured a deep-V neckline. To accent the fit of the dress, Mrs. Obama paired the sheath with a wide, black patent leather belt by Azzedine Alaïa. Completing the look was a single strand pearl necklace by Carolee. "We started to notice Mrs. Obama wearing this bold pearl style and other Carolee styles, so we knew she was an honest to goodness Carolee customer," said Karen O'Brien, vice president of worldwide marketing for Carolee. "Michelle Obama's personal style is elegant and fashionable but rooted in timeless classics, of which pearls are the epitome," she added.

The Alaïa belt had been a staple of Mrs. Obama's wardrobe; when *Vanity Fair* named Michelle Obama to their 2007 Best-Dressed List, the Alaïa belt was mentioned as a favorite accessory. Adding a substantial belt to a minimalist silk dress was an inspired choice. "The combination of that dress with that belt was amazing," said Sally Singer, of *Vogue*, in an interview with *Chicago* magazine. "Her clothes said that she was authoritative and appropriate, yet also very accessible and very refreshing."

Certainly, the belted sheath, with its bold color and exquisite fit, captured the attention of the public. That night, a fashion star—for both the fashion industry and the press—was born.

WE CAN
BELIEVE IN
IS
CHANGE
WE CAN
BELIEVE IN
CHANGE
CHANGE
WE CAN
BELIEVE IN
HANGE
VE CAN
ELIEVE IN

Maria Pinto, the Chicago-based designer, is known for her confident and sophisticated clothes, produced in clean lines and luxurious fabrics. Pinto, who studied fashion design at Chicago's School of the Art Institute and then worked for the famed designer Geoffrey Beene, calls her look "Opulent Minimalism." She is a master of bias cuts and elliptical seaming, creating body-skimming clothes that flatter many figures. Her fashion philosophy: "It's not about how much you own, it's about having a few pieces that make you look great."

In 2004, a client told her that a friend would like to come and meet her—Michelle Obama—and the rest is fashion history.

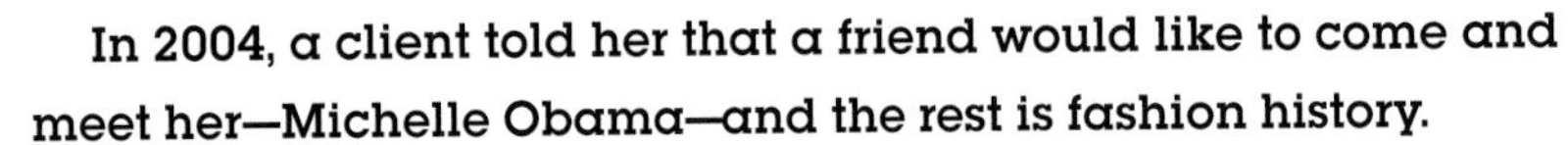

Q: How did you start working with Michelle Obama?

A: She was referred to me by another client in 2004, shortly before her husband was sworn in as a U.S. senator. She said she needed some clothes for both her work and her social life.

Q: You did evening gowns and daywear for her beginning in 2004. Were there special considerations you kept in mind?

A: Not particularly. Like all of my clients, Michelle would shop from my collections, and she would choose items that worked for her needs.

Q: The sleeveless purple silk sheath dress Michelle Obama wore has become an icon. How do you feel about that?

A: Happy, of course. And I was surprised. I didn't know she was going to wear it. I think that Michelle looks amazing in anything she wears, but she looks particularly spectacular in color. The purple sheath is a great dress because it is classic with modern seaming, and so it works for so many different body types.

Q: When she spoke on the first night at the Democratic National Convention, Mrs. Obama wore a teal dress of your design. Did you know she planned to wear it?

A: I had no idea she was going to be wearing the dress for her speech, so it was a quite a pleasant surprise! The dress was from my Fall 2008 collection; I simply chose a color that I knew she would look radiant in.

Q: Besides the purple sheath and the DNC dress, what are some of your favorite looks for her from your designs?

A: She wore the most exquisite midnight blue, high-necked halter dress with an open back to a fundraiser for the campaign at Oprah's home in Santa Barbara. The dress was hand-embellished with ribbons and beading. At the neck were sculpted flowers made of the same cut ribbons and beads as the dress. She looked simply sensational!

Also another favorite pick I would make is the Paulette dress in scarlet wool crepe, with a three-quarter sleeve and sunburst pleating at the neck. She wore it for her first visit to the White House after election night.

Q: What sparked your early interest in fashion and design?

A: I was blessed to find my calling at a young age. I had my first subscription to *Women's Wear Daily* at the age of 13. It really all began with my first sewing machine; I was making clothing for myself, which friends in turn started requesting for themselves. I even made my own prom dress from an old Halston pattern. From the beginning, I was very interested in the construction of clothes.

Scenes from inside Maria Pinto's Chicago atelier.

Q: What designers have influenced you the most?
A: Certainly working in New York for the legendary Geoffrey Beene left a major impression on my work. I credit working for Geoffrey with helping me develop my super-high standards.

Q: What inspires your design process every season?
A: For me, my inspiration can come from anything. One season it was Richard Serra's elliptical sculptures, which inspired me to do very sculptural clothes; another season it was the native costumes of Ethiopian tribes, which became all about textures and finishes and details. Once I have my inspiration for a season, I work at deconstructing it so that it isn't too literal. But for me, it is truly about beautiful fabrics and textures. I think that is what my clients have come to expect from me: gorgeous fabrics and an impeccable fit.

Q: What do you think is a defining element of Michelle Obama's style?
A: Her style is timeless. She possesses a natural sophistication. But what I love most is her brilliance and eloquence coupled by the grace and beauty of a dancer. Style aside, it is her wit and her intellect that will make her an extraordinary first lady.

Vogue & Calvin Klein Fundraiser

DRESSING FOR A HIGH FASHION CROWD MIGHT INTIMIDATE SOME, but Michelle Obama exuded confidence at this cocktail party-cum-campaign fundraiser organized by Anna Wintour and André Leon Talley of *Vogue*. She made her entrance wearing a black, front-wrapped, cigar rolled, jersey tunic and palazzo pants designed by Cuban-American designer Isabel Toledo. She added a statement necklace by Tom Binns and black open-toed patent leather high heels to the ensemble.

"She is a woman who knows exactly who she is, who just exudes warmth and friendship."

ANDRÉ LEON TALLEY, *VOGUE*

Co-hosted by communications executive Shelby Bryan and fashion designer Calvin Klein, the sold-out New York City affair featured many well-known names in the world of fashion, including Isaac Mizrahi, Tory Burch, Zac Posen, and Cynthia Rowley.

Isabel Toledo and her fashion illustrator husband, Ruben Toledo, were also present at the event, but they later said they had no idea that Mrs. Obama would be wearing one of Toledo's designs that night. "We almost fainted," Mr. Toledo told *Fashion Week Daily*.

Isabel Toledo later told *New York* magazine of meeting Michelle Obama at the event: "I have to admit, I hugged her and thought, 'Let me see . . . what size?' She's got an amazing torso and long, beautiful arms." It was an impromptu measurement that would prove fruitful during the Inauguration.

As an accent to the all black ensemble, Mrs. Obama wore a dazzling, oversized necklace by Tom Binns. It featured a bib collar of rhinestones combined with an attenuated strand of rhinestones, faux pearls, and large sea glass "gems" in red and cobalt blue. The necklace was from Binns's Nouveau Raj Collection, which he said was based on the ornately encrusted jewelry of the maharajas.

Tom Binns was born in Belfast, Northern Ireland and resides in the United States. He concentrates on taking objets trouvés—found objects like beach glass and faux gems—and reworking them into stunning, singular pieces of jewelry. He started designing in the early 1980s, first collaborating with British punk artists. His primary influence is the Dada movement, an artistic and literary philosophy that started in Switzerland in 1916 as a reaction to World War I. Dadaists believed in anarchy and deliberate irrationality, and Binns incorporates that sensibility—or lack thereof—through the unexpected mix of his materials and the oversize scale of his work.

Mrs. Obama wore a different Binns necklace—made of faux pearls and diamante—at the first black tie dinner at the Obama White House, in February 2009, and another Binns necklace—also made of beach glass and faux gems—to the Kennedy Center in March 2009.

The View

FOR HER GUEST CO-HOST APPEARANCE ON *THE VIEW*, the award-winning daytime talk show on ABC, Michelle Obama wore a black and white, high-waisted print dress designed by Donna Ricco. Sleeveless and form-fitting, the cotton dress featured a low scoop neck and a double band of black trim—one band encircling the empire waistline and the other at the natural waist. To accessorize the graphic leaf print, Mrs. Obama pinned a large black and silver peony-like brooch high on one shoulder. During the live broadcast, she confided that while she sometimes does wear "high-end clothes," she had purchased this dress at White House Black Market, a national chain store. "You put a little pin on it, and you've got something going on," she said.

"She was still on the air when our phones—both in our corporate headquarters and in our stores across the country—started ringing non-stop," said Jessica Wells, director of public relations for White House Black Market, in an interview with *Chicago* magazine. The dress, which retailed for $148.00, sold out across the country within 48 hours. It was purchased by women of all sizes and all ages, and orders for the next shipment—arriving in three months—quickly mounted. White House Black Market featured the dress on its Web site, under the headline, "Road to the White House Style." Appearing on the *Today* show two days later to discuss the popularity of the dress, Ricco assured shoppers that "we're making more dresses as fast as we can."

Mrs. Obama's choice of this dress was her public debut of a high-low chic ensemble, and it fueled a growing national interest in her style. While she discussed her sense of patriotism, her working class upbringing, and her dislike of panty hose on *The View*, her legacy from this appearance was her emerging status as a fashion icon.

Summer

Donna Ricco **is known for her affordable range of chic, zip-and-go dresses. In the early summer of 2008, Michelle Obama wore a black and white print Donna Ricco dress for an appearance on *The View*. She announced that she had bought the dress from the store that sells "black and white clothes"—White House Black Market—instantaneously creating a fashion frenzy.**

Q: How did you get started as a designer?

A: I came to New York right after I graduated with my bachelor of arts in fashion design. I had met my future husband in Milwaukee a year before that. We had decided to join forces and come to New York. Neither of us had a job, and we just said, "Let's see what we can get into."

Q: Where was your first order?

A: Henri Bendel. It was eight pieces, and it was very exciting. It was back in the day when young designers could go and show their ideas to the buyers directly. They had an open call.

Q: What do you like about dresses in particular?

A: As a designer, I always look at a dress as a complete statement. I think that's part of the artist in me. You buy it, you put it on, and you're ready to go. Yes, you can add a belt or put on accessories, but still, you're covered head to toe. It's really pure, and I like that idea.

Q: Did you know Michelle Obama owned one of your dresses?

A: I had no idea; it was a complete surprise. I was working, and we got a call from White House Black Market. When she was on *The View*, she said she bought it at the store that sells "black and white clothes." They started getting calls from customers and the media, things happened so quickly. My husband Tom said, "Hey, I just got this call. Michelle Obama's wearing your dress on *The View*." When he said that, my heart, it just jumped.

Q: Why do you think there was so much excitement around *The View* dress?

A: It really speaks to the power of the dress—a good dress. That was what was so pure and so wonderful about the whole experience. I put so much effort into every dress that I design, and it's something that I've been doing for so many years, since I started.

For so many people to react in such a positive way—it was the right cut, the right fit, the right print, and she bought it off the rack. Everything was right about it.

Q: The fit really was very flattering.

A: It has those black bands in the midriff area. A lot of my dresses have that fitted waist detail. Most women have a good shape there and like to show off that part of their body. And many American women are fuller in the hips. That dress has a slight A-line cut, and the fact that it had a higher waist—it just fit her figure perfectly.

Q: What impact might Michelle Obama have on the way American women look at fashion?

A: I think women will reach out a little more to something more current in fashion. They'll think about wearing something other than a suit for daytime. It was a daytime event that Michelle Obama was attending. Because she wore it with such confidence, I think she's a good role model for so many women in America. I think that's good inspiration for all of us. The fact that she bought it off the rack from a store that anyone could walk into—I think that was really positive.

Black and white print dress by Donna Ricco, worn by Michelle Obama on *The View*.

Washington, D.C.

FOR HER APPEARANCE at the annual luncheon hosted by the National Partnership for Women & Families, Michelle Obama chose a suit by Narciso Rodriguez, a designer known for modern, streamlined designs executed in the most luxurious of fabrics. The short boxy jacket featured a moderate scoop neckline and three-quarter sleeves, while the coordinating dress underneath was slim and straight.

The eye-catching material showcased horizontal bands of gray and white, with the gray bands varying in size and gradations of color. Serving as a counterpoint to the strong geometric look of the suit was a lush feather and crystal pin by Carolyn Rosenberg. The pin, with its gathered plumage of purple feathers held in place by a curving black jet-encrusted leaf, added an airy, feminine touch. Both the suit and the pin were acquired through the boutique Ikram.

The son of Cuban immigrants, designer Narciso Rodriguez grew up in New Jersey and pursued work in the fashion industry both in the U.S. and Europe. He worked for established labels such as Anne Klein and Calvin Klein, but he achieved instant stardom in 1996 by designing a sleek and sophisticated dress for Carolyn Bessette's wedding to John F. Kennedy Jr.

Carolyn Rosenberg, a Chicago-based jewelry designer, was commissioned by boutique owner Ikram Goldman to make this pin specifically for Michelle Obama. (Mrs. Obama later wore this pin during her October 8, 2008, interview on *The Larry King Live Show* on CNN.)

Ms. Rosenberg inherited a collection of vintage items from an aunt who had been a milliner, which would become the basis for her first collection of jewelry. "I was taken with the idea of repurposing beautiful items, and I had these wonderful feathers from my aunt. They had been dyed with vegetable dye in the 1920s and '30s, and the dying was beautiful. I also had all of these little jet pieces that had been soldered onto wires—these, too, were part of my aunt's collection. Originally, they were for decorations on hats or for pins. So my approach was, 'How can I get these things that I love to work together?'"

In her speech at the luncheon, Michelle Obama addressed some of the unique challenges facing America's working families, including an expansion of family leave, health care reform and equality of wages. "I've always been and will probably always be in some way, shape, or form, a working mom," she said. This was one of Mrs. Obama's first public appearance wearing Rodriguez, but his designs would become one of her wardrobe staples.

ABOVE: Purple feather brooch, made of dyed, vintage feathers and jet pieces, by Carolyn Rosenberg of Chicago.

Butte, MO

FRIDAY, JULY 4, 2008

THE OBAMAS CELEBRATED INDEPENDENCE DAY with the citizens of Butte, Montana. Arriving in town to watch the annual holiday parade, Mrs. Obama wore a blue and white windowpane sundress from Gap. At first, Mrs. Obama wore a white cardigan over the cotton sundress, but she soon removed the sweater and tied it around her shoulders. She also added an impomptu accessory—a beaded Native American rosette necklace, handed to her by someone in the crowd.

On the most American of holidays, Mrs. Obama made a pitch perfect pick by wearing an inexpensive off-the-rack dress from all-American brand Gap. "General joy," is how Gap's creative director, Patrick Robinson, descibed his reaction, adding "All Gap employees felt that." Commenting on the choice of dress for the occasion, he continued, "Gap has a long heritage in America; it is the iconic American brand. So it seemed appropriate that she wore it."

Started 40 years ago in San Francisco, Gap has concentrated on producing all-American basics like jeans, T-shirts and cardigan sweaters. The embodiment of fashion democracy, Gap has fashioned its brand on making affordable, classically casual sportswear. Before joining Gap in 2007, Mr. Robinson had worked at Giorgio Armani, Anne Klein, Perry Ellis, and Paco Rabanne. Now leading the affordable retailer, he remarked, "Michelle Obama seems to understand fashion, and she wears clothes for the look and the design, rather than just going with high-price labels. She's willing to embrace fashion wherever she finds it."

Springfield, IL

THE ANNOUNCEMENT OF SENATOR OBAMA'S RUNNING MATE—Joseph Biden, the senior senator from Delaware—came at 3 AM via a posting on the campaign's Web site and text messages to supporters.

So by the time the Obamas stepped off their plane for an afternoon rendezvous and a pubic rally in Springfield, Illinois, with the Bidens, the excitement in the state capital town had been building. A crowd of 35,000 people jammed the streets surrounding the historic Old State Capitol to welcome the presumptive presidential and vice presidential candidates and their families. According to the *Springfield Journal-Register*, many in the crowd had driven hours or caught an Amtrak train from other cities in order to witness the event. The rally was a kickoff to the Democratic National Convention that was five days away.

Mrs. Obama was dressed for the sultry summer weather in a colorful shirtwaist dress by Moschino. In tones of deep purple, moss green, and blue gray, the floral print—which resembled impressionistic irises—was a cool counterpoint to the temperature.

Rossella Jardini of Moschino, describes the fabric: "In this beautiful print the flower can be seen although it is not clearly defined. The colors are not superimposed but integrated, almost mixed, without a determinate base color. This print is born of the simple fantasy and spontaneous coming together of joyous colors."

The silhouette of the dress, with its short sleeves, button front, and slightly rounded shoulders, recalls vintage fashion of the 1940s. As an unexpected twist on the classic style, the placket curves asymmetrically with one side of the shirt front gathering to tie with an attached sash at the side of the waist. Tiered folds accent the loose, flowing skirt.

Watercolor blue, floral shirtdress from Moschino's Spring 2008 collection.

CHAPTER III DEMOCRATIC NATIONAL CONVENTION

Making an Entrance

At the time of the 2008 Democratic National Convention, many Americans were still just getting to know Michelle Obama. It was during the convention that she would step onto the national stage, giving Americans an opportunity to connect with her on a more personal level. Quickly they would realize her warmth, commitment to her husband's campaign, and, of course, her captivating, iconic style.

The convention was a weeklong affair held in Denver, Colorado, during August 2008, consisting of both day and evening activities. While Michelle Obama would make a prime-time speech and host a large service effort, her presence was undeniably felt through her style as well. The week proved to be one of Mrs. Obama's most rigorously, well-styled efforts, in great part thanks to the discerning eye of Ikram Goldman, who served as a behind-the-scenes fashion advisor.

With each passing night, Mrs. Obama's fashion choices seemed to grow more chic: the unexpected choice of designers, the clever use of accessories, the confidence and ease with which she wore each ensemble. There was an unparalleled thoughtfulness and cohesive attention to detail with each look that made for a dramatic, lasting impact. It was during this week that many American women—this author included—found themselves captivated with Michelle Obama's style.

"Michelle Obama was so integral to the landscape of American fashion from the first moment she hit the campaign spotlight with her husband," said Joe Zee, creative director of *Elle* magazine. "Here was this incredibly chic, well-respected, smart and not to mention—beautiful—woman that represented all the integrity and foundations of every woman in this country, and all eyes were on her."

First Night of the Convention

AS AN INSTRUMENTAL VERSION of Stevie Wonder's "Isn't She Lovely" filled the air and thousands of delegates joyfully waved "Michelle" signs, Michelle Obama was set to take the stage of the 2008 Democratic National Convention at the Pepsi Center in Denver.

A biographical video "Michelle Obama: South Side Girl," narrated by Michelle's mother, Marian Robinson, had played just minutes before, tracing Michelle's childhood years on Chicago's South Side, to meeting Barack Obama at the Chicago law firm Sidley Austin, to her later work at Public Allies and the University of Chicago.

Michelle's brother, Craig Robinson, gave his younger sister a warm, energetic introduction before the evening's headline speaker finally walked on stage.

For her prime-time appearance, Mrs. Obama chose a teal, three-quarter sleeve, sheath dress created by Chicago designer Maria Pinto. With its fitted, fifties-inspired shape in double-faced wool, the dress conveyed an easy, understated elegance. At the center of its draped neckline, Mrs. Obama pinned an oversize turquoise starburst brooch with a silver rose center designed by Erickson Beamon. The brooch added personalized punctuation to the outfit, a winning combination that would become a trademark of Mrs. Obama's style. Simple black patent leather pumps completed her outfit.

For designer Maria Pinto, the choice of dress confirmed her status as one of Mrs. Obama's signature designers, a coveted position on the path to the White House. That same month, the designer had opened her first boutique in Chicago's West Loop district.

Poised and confident, Mrs. Obama addressed the crowd for 20 minutes, speaking fondly of her brother, father, and mother, of the joys of being a mother herself, of her husband and the kind of president she believed he would become. After sharing a story about the day she and Barack Obama drove home from the hospital with their newborn daughter Malia, Mrs. Obama spoke these words of inspiration:

"As I tuck that little girl and her little sister into bed at night, you see, I think about how one day, they'll have families of their own and how one day, they—and your sons and daughters—will tell their own children about

LEFT: Erickson Beamon Victory Garden brooch in turquoise and oxidized silver plated metal.

RIGHT: Teal V-neck sheath dress by Maria Pinto.

what we did together in this election. They'll tell them how this time we listened to our hopes, instead of our fears . . . how this time, we decided to stop doubting and to start dreaming . . . how this time, in this great country, where a girl from the South Side of Chicago can go to college and law school, and the son of a single mother from Hawaii can go all the way to the White House . . . that we committed ourselves . . . to building the world as it should be."

Following the speech, Mrs. Obama was joined onstage by her two young, jubilant daughters: Malia, wearing an empire waist sundress in black and cobalt blue, and Sasha, wearing a short sleeve purple shift dress adorned with a white flower pin.

Barack Obama appeared on a large screen via satellite from Kansas City, Missouri, where he was spending the evening. "Hello from Kansas City," he said. And in praise of his wife: "How about Michelle Obama!"

THE LUNCHEON FOR LGBT CAUCUS DELEGATES, hosted by Rep. Barney Frank of Massachusetts and Rep. Tammy Baldwin of Wisconsin, included a surprise visit: an unscheduled appearance and short speech by Michelle Obama. Delegates welcomed Mrs. Obama to the luncheon with roaring applause.

LGBT Caucus

"We know our country's journey toward equality is not finished yet," Mrs. Obama said. "We know it right here in this room. It's been five years since *Lawrence v. Texas* and 39 years since *Stonewall*, but still, we've got work to do before we achieve equality in the LGBT community. And although we know we have a lot of work to do, this week we are going to celebrate just how far we've come, and how deep our shared capacity is to break through any barriers that stand in our way to the progress of this nation."

Following her speech, Mrs. Obama stepped down from the stage to greet delegates, projecting understated elegance in a medley of earth tones and her trademark metallic ballet flats. Mrs. Obama wore an accordion pleat dress in taupe linen by Rodarte, belted at the waist with a coordinating taupe sash. A trio of Japanese glass pearl necklaces in bronze, gold, and champagne from the Erickson Beamon Peace at Last collection complemented the look.

Rodarte was founded in 2005 by two sisters, Kate and Laura Mulleavy. Rodarte is also their mother's maiden name, chosen for their label as a tribute to their mother and grandfather. Their rise in American fashion has been meteoric; in June 2008, just two months before Michelle Obama chose the dress from their Fall 2007 collection, Rodarte received the CFDA Swarovski Emerging Womenswear designer award. Recognition of young design talent would be an emerging theme in Michelle Obama's wardrobe, an early example of which was notably seen here. Michelle Obama would later re-wear the same dress as first lady, for her meeting with Queen Rania of Jordan at the White House in April 2009.

That same afternoon, Mrs. Obama also spoke at the Emily's List Convention gala, and at the Women's Economic Roundtable event with Sentaor Joe Biden.

"Whenever a woman accessorizes, she puts her own point of view on a look. If you accessorize with your own creativity, you're putting your own stamp on an individual look."

KAREN ERICKSON, ERICKSON BEAMON

Erickson Beamon Peace at Last necklace made of Japanese glass pearls and oxidized silver plated metal.

TUESDAY, AUGUST 26, 2008

FOR THE SECOND NIGHT OF THE DEMOCRATIC NATIONAL CONVENTION, the night Hillary Clinton addressed the convention in a prime-time speech, Mrs. Obama watched and listened attentively from the audience.

The previous evening, Michelle Obama had described Hillary Clinton, her husband's former opponent in the primary campaign, as a woman "who put those 18 million cracks in that glass ceiling so that our daughters and our sons can dream a little bigger and aim a little higher."

Second Night of the Convention

Seated between vice presidential candidate Joe Biden to her left, and her mother, Marian Robinson, to her right, the future first lady was a vision of poise and youthful grace.

The sequel to Mrs. Obama's teal Maria Pinto sheath dress proved to be another sartorial standout: a romantic, feminine cocktail dress by Peter Soronen. The ivory and lime rose-patterned brocade cocktail dress was custom made for Mrs. Obama, using fabric from Soronen's Pre-Spring 2008 collection, and cut in a dress design from his Fall 2008 collection. The original dress included three-quarter length balloon sleeves and a deep scoop neckline, but was altered for Mrs. Obama—the sleeves shortened to above the elbow and a ruffle added at the bust, presumably for modesty. Lime piping defined the empire waist and original neckline.

Mrs. Obama complemented the dress with a soft updo, her bangs swept to the side, and drop citrine stone earrings.

TOP: Ivory and lime rose-patterned brocade used in Peter Soronen's Pre-Spring 2008 collection.

ABOVE: Peter Soronen dress before alteration.

RIGHT: Michelle Obama pictured with her brother Craig Robinson and former President Jimmy Carter.

PRIORITY MAIL
UNITED STATES POSTAL SERVICE
SAVE MORE $ BY SHIPPING ONLINE

WEDNESDAY, AUGUST 27, 2008

Delegate Service Day

A LONGTIME CHAMPION OF PUBLIC SERVICE, Michelle Obama was named the co-chair of the Democratic National Convention's Delegate Service Day, along with Jeannie Ritter, the first lady of Colorado. Mrs. Obama joined volunteers who planted trees in Denver's Curtis Park and put together care packages for troops overseas, while a broader service effort cascaded across the city.

In an opinion piece co-written for the *Denver Post* in advance of the Service Day, Mrs. Obama and Mrs. Ritter encouraged participation:

"Our nation is built on a history of service, written by generations of soldiers and sailors, suffragists and freedom riders, teachers and doctors, police officers and firefighters. Their lesson to us is simple but profound: In America, each of us is free to seek our own dreams, but we must also serve a common and higher purpose."

Standing on a stage in front of an expansive American flag, Mrs. Obama opened Delegate Service Day with a speech to volunteers. Like those serving, she wore a blue "Supporting Our Troops" T-shirt, rolling up her sleeves for the day, literally and figuratively. The look was kept casual with black capri pants and open toe black flats.

SUPPORTING
OUR
TROOPS

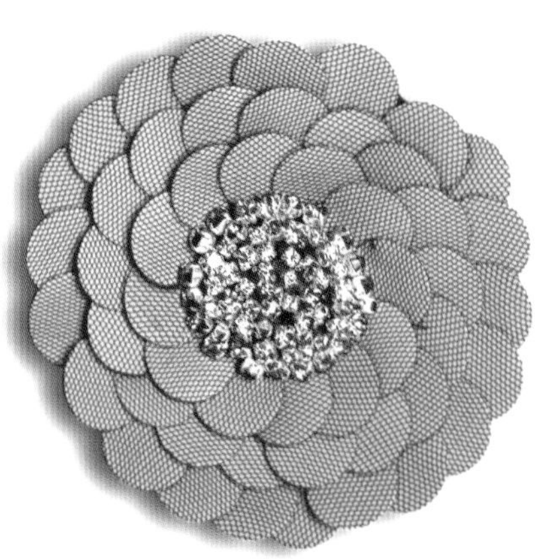

WEDNESDAY, AUGUST 27, 2008

SEATED IN THE AUDIENCE BETWEEN BARACK OBAMA'S GREAT-UNCLE, veteran Charlie Payne, and Teresa Heinz Kerry, wife of 2004 presidential candidate John Kerry, Mrs. Obama jumped to her feet in applause at the conclusion of vice presidential candidate Joe Biden's impassioned speech.

Third Night of the Convention

Mrs. Obama's face was aglow from the reflected sparkle of four floral brooches, placed at the round neckline of her azure blue silk dress by Narciso Rodriguez. While at first glance the embellishments appeared to be part of the dress design, they were in fact four distinct pins, inventively added to accessorize.

Resembling Blue Bell dahlias, each pin has layers of finely articulated sequin petals and a shimmering center of tiny metallic beads, which combine to add beautiful movement and dimension to the design. Designed by Rossella Jardini, creative director of Moschino, the pins were featured in the Italian design house's Fall 2008 collection, where single brooches were placed at the neck of high collar, ruffled white shirts.

When asked about the use of brooches in her recent collections, Rossella Jardini replied, "Brooches? Yes, I love them. I perceive them as the accents on specific words in the fashion language: they are the guidelines for the proper reading of the full sentence. A particular style changes depending upon the type of brooch, where they are placed, and how evident or camouflaged they are on the dress or jacket."

LEFT:
Brooches from Moschino's Fall 2008 collection.

THURSDAY, AUGUST 28, 2008

Final Day of the Convention

TO BEGIN THE FINAL DAY OF THE DEMOCRATIC NATIONAL CONVENTION, Michelle Obama chose an understated navy blue V-neck dress for a speaking engagement at the Women's Caucus and a television interview with CBS's Katie Couric.

At first glance, the dress may have appeared to be a simple shift dress, but a closer look revealed hidden detail and fine craftsmanship—the work of Isabel Toledo. The fitted bodice was created by two bands of fabric that encircle the waist, while exposed seams run the length of the A-line skirt, adding nuanced detail. An amaryllis-inspired brooch pinned at the center the neckline brought a feminine embellishment.

Describing her design process, Isabel Toledo explains, "All types of cuts create emotion in a garment. Where is the knee showing? Where do you feel it tight on you? You're aware of the garment according to how it fits you. Your body language becomes important. You use your body in a way according to the dress. I think of all of these things before I design. I think of the lines according to that."

In the final minutes of Mrs. Obama's interview with Katie Couric, conversation shifted to the role of first ladies. "Somebody asked me, 'Is there a standard notion of what a first lady should be?'" said Mrs. Obama. "If you look at Eleanor Roosevelt, Jacqueline Kennedy, Barbara Bush, Laura Bush—they have all been in some way uniquely non-traditional. . . . And the country received each and every one of those women with a level of openness and possibility. I hope to learn from each of them if I have the honor of being the next first lady of the United States."

Final Night of the Convention

FOR THE FINAL NIGHT OF THE DEMOCRATIC NATIONAL CONVENTION, the evening Barack Obama would accept his party's nomination for president, Mile High Stadium in Denver, Colorado, was packed with thousands of enthusiastic delegates and campaign supporters.

Making her boldest style statement of the week, Mrs. Obama wore an abstract floral print cocktail dress that would at once send the inner circles of the fashion community abuzz, while enchanting style-conscious women across the country. In a single ensemble, Mrs. Obama set herself on an almost certain, though likely unintended, path toward becoming a style icon.

The dress was the work of Thakoon Panichgul, a young, talented New York designer whose eponymous line, Thakoon, had launched to critical acclaim just four years prior. The dress, a reverse kimono-style design in a graphic cabbage rose print, hailed from the designer's yet-to-be-released Resort 2009 collection. Mrs. Obama had purchased the dress in late July from the Chicago boutique Ikram, after Ikram Goldman had requested an early shipment of cocktail dresses from Thakoon for a "special client."

Mrs. Obama was widely applauded in the media for demonstrating an astute, modern fashion sensibility with her choice of dress and designer. In fact, it was at least the second time Mrs. Obama had worn the reverse kimono dress design from Thakoon. Named such for its crossover V-back

with tie waist belt, the dress originally appeared in Thakoon's Spring 2007 collection in a black silk cotton crinkled fabric, selling out when it debuted at Bergdorf Goodman in 2007. Mrs. Obama previously wore the dress in black for a campaign fundraiser in September 2007.

Mr. Panichgul described his reaction to learning the future first lady had chosen his design in the February 2009 issue of *Harper's Bazaar*: "I had no idea," Panichgul said. "I was so shocked and honored to have been part of that moment for her, for her family, for the country."

The dress was not the only style star of the night. In lieu of a necklace, Mrs. Obama chose a trio of brooches by Erickson Beamon, pinned at the neckline of her dress. In scarlet, lilac, and gray, each brooch featured a rose center surrounded by clusters of small pearls and stones, mirroring the print and colors of her dress's fabric.

Following Barack Obama's speech, Mrs. Obama and daughters Malia and Sasha, joined the nominee on stage. The girls pink and white summer dresses—Malia's a lace empire waist sundress and Sasha's an ombré-effect bubble dress—were a perfect complement to their mother's. As the family walked to the front of the stage, waving to the vast audience, fashion observers also took note of Mrs. Obama's shoes. Instead of heels, Mrs. Obama chose sensible black flats, signaling as she would so many times in the future, that she would make her own style rules.

Front (left) and back (right) of Thakoon's reverse kimono dress in cabbage rose print.

Karen Erickson, of New York City, is one half of the jewelry design duo Erickson Beamon; her creative partner, Vicki Beamon, resides in London. Together, they run the highly successful "baubles-and-bangles empire" with more than 25 years in business together. Through the years they've collaborated with an impressive range of design houses from Dior to Chanel to Anna Sui, and attracted a long of list high-profile clientele—including one that is a great source of pride: Michelle Obama.

Q: How did you get into jewelry design?

A: I actually first started by making crazy, whacked-out snakeskin platform shoes in the '70s—and selling them to all of the fabulous rock and rollers who lived in Detroit at the time. That's how I got into the fashion business, and I've sort of been in it ever since.

Q: So how did the jewelry eventually come about?

A: It was 1983. Vicki Beamon and I were making clothing, and we needed jewelry for a runway show, so we started making jewelry. We strung crystals on suede.

At the fashion show—everyone was more interested in the jewelry than the clothes. We sold to Barneys and Bergdorf the next day. Joan Weinstein [former owner of Ultimo in Chicago] bought our first jewelry collection in '83 as well.

Q: What's the core essence of your collection?

A: I'm interested in the beauty of the piece, or the story I'm telling with it. I'm not limited or directed by any fine jewelry mystique. I don't think diamonds or rubies are better. I would certainly mix a ruby with a crystal.

I want all the raw materials to have integrity, but it's the craftsmanship that goes into the pieces that's important. And for me, a lot of it is people who make it. I work very closely in the design room, and in our production room, with each piece.

Q: Do you have a most treasured piece of jewelry?

A: I don't own anything. In fact, look, I have nothing on. For me, when I design, it's theoretical. It's for this person, or this composition, or this idea, or this statement that I want to make. It's never about what I want to wear to a party on Thursday night.

Q: What's the appeal of brooches?

A: I think maybe a brooch is the easiest thing you can wear. I mean you feel earrings, and your necklace is there. And a brooch, you sort of put it on, and you no longer deal with it. It becomes a part of the dress.

Monique Erickson (Karen's daughter, and Erickson Beamon brand director): As Michelle Obama wore them, clipping brooches onto a pearl necklace [for one of the presidential debates], it dressed up a more conservative look.

It brought an edge—it was a creative input that made everything look more creative.

Q: What do you think Michelle Obama's jewelry adds to her style?

A: Well I think whenever a woman accessorizes she puts her own point of view on a look. If you just buy things without accessories, you're usually just taking the designer's point of view. If you accessorize with your own creativity, you're putting your own stamp on an individual look. Americans don't want to look so cookie cutter. I think that's why people respond so much to Michelle Obama—she has a personality, she's a strong woman. And I think right now, we want a strong woman.

Q: The brooches from the Democratic National Convention, for example, were they designed to be worn together?

A: In my mind I always wanted them clustered—to have a beautiful garden feeling. They're part of a collection called Victory Garden.

Q: The First Lady has worn Erickson Beamon glass pearls that were part of a collection called Peace at Last.

A: We wanted the Obamas to win. It was Peace at Last, because we wanted to put our energy into them winning, so that we could have some peace, at last.

Q: I thought perhaps I was reading too much into the names.

A: You were not.

Erickson Beamon Victory Garden brooches featuring vintage Bakelite flowers.

Thakoon Panichgul is a Thai-born, Omaha-raised American fashion designer. He started his career as a merchandiser for J.Crew, before he took a job as a features assistant at *Harper's Bazaar*. From there, he attended Parsons, starting his own critically-acclaimed line upon graduation. Michelle Obama is a fan of his work, wearing his designs long before the world began following her fashion.

Q: Where does a new collection begin for you?
A: I fixate on a single detail, or an idea. And then I work around that. The idea could be from an art show, or a movie, or a person. For me it's more tactile. I go to a lot of galleries; I look at a lot of photography; and I certainly look to the street. In Tokyo, there's always inspiration. And then I fixate on an idea and go from there—maybe I'll focus on the shoulder, or the waist, or the bodice. Then I start to drape on a [mannequin] form.

Q: Your collections consistently include rose prints.
A: I like prints in general, but I have a special relationship with the rose. It's kind of a love-hate relationship. It's such a clichéd symbol of romance, but then it's such a wonderful flower. When you look at it a certain way, it can even become erotic. The rose can take on so many different forms and mean so many different things to different people. But when Valentine's Day comes around, everyone—chic women and tacky women alike—wants a rose. I like the multi-faceted dimensions of that flower.

Q: Last fall you told the *New York Times* that you like to create silhouettes that have a "built-in gesture." What did you mean by that?
A: I like the idea that an article of clothing can make a woman act a certain way, or feel a certain way, all because of the way that the clothes fall off the body. Maybe it makes you stand a certain way. A good example is the dress that Mrs. Obama wore to the closing night of the Democratic National Convention. The back of that dress is a low open back which, when you cinch tight at the waist, allows the shoulders to fall off. Then there are pockets. So between the shoulders and the pockets, the wearer forms this gesture, and your body takes on this cool posture.

Q: You seem to like to do things the other way around: the reverse kimono from the DNC, the inside-out dress that Mrs. Obama wore for the first debate. Is there a reason behind that?
A: I grew up loving more avant garde designers, minimalism and Helmut Lang. I like examining ideas of a garment, looking at its deconstruction—but not in a fussy way. I like to take patterns apart and examine them, and see why they've been created that way, highlight the seams and twist them. What happens when you wear it backwards? Or upside down? At the end of the day, they're built-in ideas about clothes, and they're secondary to the actual garment. They're never screaming. You don't recognize them right off the bat.

Q: What was your reaction upon learning Michelle Obama had worn your dress on the final night of the DNC? How did you find out?
A: I got home from work and turned the convention on the television. I had been watching the speeches all week. I had known that she had bought the dress from Ikram, but I didn't know when she was going to wear it, or if she would. I saw the first few nights that she was in solid colors, so I thought she didn't want a print for this convention.

The first image I saw was of her with her daughter on her lap, and I could see the top part of what she was wearing. And I could see my print. That's when I kind of freaked out. I thought, "That can't be! That can't be!"

Q: Do you think that she is now America's style icon?
A: I think what she is doing is great for fashion, and I love that she's shifting gears from celebrity culture. It's great that the person whose fashion we're celebrating is a working mother. I look up to her for who she is. But yes, if she's not already considered one, Michelle Obama will be an icon.

Medley of roses by Miho Kosuda, Ltd., Thakoon's favorite New York City florist. "What I love about roses is the process of blooming and wilting," Panichgul told *W* magazine in November 2008, "and Miho's roses die so beautifully."

CHAPTER IV PRESIDENTIAL CAMPAIGN

Declaration of Fashion Independence

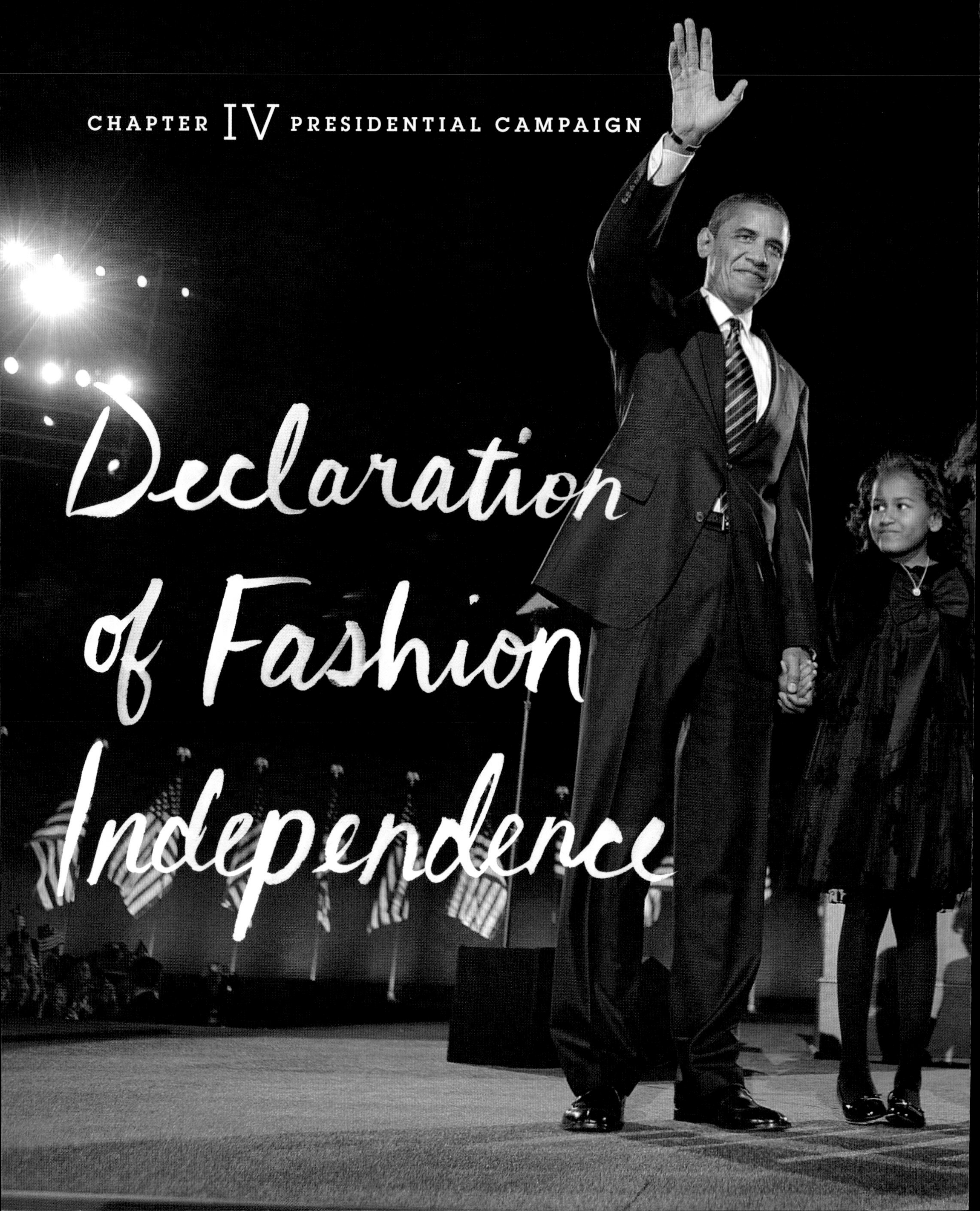

After stepping gracefully into the spotlight during the Democratic National Convention, Michelle Obama continued to move onto a national stage during the presidential race. While she was often seen accompanying her husband at events, or providing moral support from the audience during the presidential debates, Mrs. Obama also continued her many solo campaign speaking roles.

It was during this time that she began to show more fashion confidence, even at times, daring in her sartorial choices. While she continued to wear clothes by her hometown favorite designer, Maria Pinto, she increasingly began to move toward other designers: Narciso Rodriguez, Maria Cornejo, and Jason Wu, for example. Mrs. Obama came to these designers by building a fashion partnership that can be summed up in one word: Ikram.

That is the definitively fashionable Chicago boutique named after its glamorous owner, Ikram Goldman. Aside from Maria Pinto, the brightest fashion influence on Michelle Obama has been Goldman. Ikram expands the fashion possibilities for anyone who shops there. In Chicago, the boutique is known as the place where women can discover their inner chic selves.

During this time period, Mrs. Obama also began to integrate more readily available, affordable clothing into her wardrobe, appearing for high profile events in ensembles by J.Crew and H&M. On *The Tonight Show*, she talked of how convenient it was to shop online. But even to off-the-rack or off-the-net clothing, she always added her own personal touch, usually jewelry—sometimes using vintage pieces for a unique look.

At first, these two fashion styles—cutting edge fashion insiders or retail wear—may seem at odds with each other. In fact, they mirror what has become known in the fashion industry as "high-low style." It is a democratic approach to fashion that Michelle Obama has famously embraced.

WEDNESDAY, SEPTEMBER 24, 2008

Philadelphia, PA

MICHELLE OBAMA AND JILL BIDEN joined Pennsylvania Governor Ed Rendell and Philadelphia Mayor Michael Nutter for a campaign rally in South West Philadelphia, which drew more than 3,000 people to the grounds of the Francis J. Myers Recreation Center. Mrs. Obama and Mrs. Biden appeared at ease, sitting on wooden stools as they addressed the crowd.

"Look at this time as an opportunity for change," said Mrs. Obama. "In forty days, we get the chance to put Barack Obama in the White House." The timing of the rally was strategic: onlookers were encouarged to help with a late voter registration effort before the state's October 6 deadline.

Mrs. Obama was smartly dressed for the event, wearing a tailored black jacket by Zero + Maria Cornejo, cut in evening raffia fabric. Known for her skilled draping, Maria Cornejo brings her own unique aesthetic to her tailoring as well. As seen in this jacket, minimalist lines—a round neckline, clean placket, and three-quarter length sleeves—create an unfussy, structured piece. The absence of a shoulder seam allows the jacket to follow the body's natural lines, flattering the shape of the wearer.

Pairing the jacket with black pants and flats, Mrs. Obama put her personal stamp on the ensemble, adding a patent leather belt at the waist and two oversize, graphic floral pins at the neck. Mrs. Obama, who also owns the jacket in a textured blue wool, would wear the black jacket a second time for a White House event in March 2009.

CHANGE
WE NEED
CHANGE

Maria Cornejo is a Chilean-born, UK-raised, New York–based fashion designer. Her accent reflects her unique upbringing, revealing hints of Spanish and British in conversation. As a child, she moved with her parents from Chile to London, where she attended school and developed her career as a designer. She later lived for ten years in Paris before relocating, in 1996, to New York, where she opened her store and atelier, Zero + Maria Cornejo, on Mott St. (In 2009, she relocated to a larger space on Bleecker Street, between Lafayette and Bowery.)

Her clothes have a strong signature and loyal following, known for their geometric reference, thoughtful draping and thorough attention to the female form. First Lady Michelle Obama has become a fan, wearing Zero + Maria Cornejo dresses and tailored jackets over the past several years.

Q: How did your interest in fashion first develop?
A: When I was a kid [in Chile], I used to make my doll clothes. My grandmother taught me how to knit on big carpenter's nails, because my grandfather did construction. I used to sit with her and knit. It was a nice way of doing things quietly. And my aunts used to always be making their own clothes; I was very influenced by them.

Q: How did fashion school come about?
A: When I was at school [in England], I started working at a fashion store called Elle, which was quite well known at the time. They sold designer clothes and owned the Issey Miyake boutique in London. My Saturday job was to wash the hangers, get everybody's lunch and wear all the ugly outfits that nobody was buying because I was young and cute—or so they said to me. I got really interested in it all. I just thought it was fascinating.

From there, I decided to go to fashion school. I got a diploma in graphics, but geared toward fashion, so I was doing magazine covers, lettering and graphics. I think some of that influence is still in my clothing—the fact that it's very graphic. Then later, I went into fashion and textiles at Ravensbourne College in London.

Q: And from there, how did your business develop?
A: I sold my college collection to Joseph and Whistles [boutiques in London], which was unique at the time. The collection was called "Urban Cowboys Clash in 3-D"; it was denim, bright blue, florescent green, nylon. It was mad. It was all of this denim mixed up with nylon raincoats, mixed up with wool knits.

I was sewing clothes in my little apartment with no heating, dying zippers in the bathtub, cutting things out on the floor, and getting on the bus from Bricklane to Clapham with boxes full of zippers and buttons. Not very glamorous, but fun.

Later, I decided to go into business with my partner at the time, John Richmond. So we called it Richmond Cornejo. We had a lot of press. We had a Japanese licensee. Joseph [a major London retailer] opened a store for us in London, first on Bond St. then on Brompton Rd. With the Japanese licensee, we had more than 20 stores by the time I was 23. We were like rock stars in Japan, with hoards of kids asking for our autographs.

Q: What do you think got you so far, so soon?
A: The whole scene was very vibrant at the time. Everything was happening together—magazines, music, fashion, retail, and of course, the nightclubs. I think also coming after punk, we were all pretty naive; so we were all just going for it. Most of us in London at the time just wanted to do something interesting. Nobody was really that business minded; it all sort of happened by accident.

Q: How have the places you've lived and spent a lot of time in—Chile, London, Milan, Paris, Tokyo, New York—influenced you?

A: The main thing, for me, is that it has taught me how to be very insular in a way. You have to be as a designer, in order to have an identity. You can see there's a little bit of English eccentricity and always a sense of humor. I worked in Japan, and so yeah, my work can be quite minimal. And I love vibrant color, which I suppose could come from my Latin American childhood. I don't look for these influences in any way, but I'm sure they're all in here somewhere, and my brain is constantly sorting them and spewing them out again.

Q: Can you describe your design process?

A: It always starts with the fabrics. I pick fabrics for their beauty and for the fact that they do something interesting. The fabric takes a shape or drapes in a particular way. Once it's on the body, it transforms. It's always about the woman's body and how to flatter a woman.

We start with a drawing, usually a little scribble, like a chicken scratching, but then it gets draped and it gets tweaked before being made into a muslin, a sample, and finally a finished pattern. It's always an evolution. I think that's why the clothes work, because they're very much about the form, about the body—it's not just an abstract idea. I have to say, in order for the clothes to look that laid-back, I torture myself a lot. There's a lot of torture that goes into getting the perfect dress that looks effortless.

Q: What's your approach to tailoring?

A: I like things with no real shoulder seams usually. I feel like it's a lot kinder to a woman's figure. The shoulder follows a natural line. That sleeve that Michelle Obama has been wearing, basically anyone can wear. It's about where your shape fits into it. It doesn't matter if you've got little shoulders or big shoulders, the jacket will look good, and it will make your arms look skinnier and longer.

Q: What kind of women are attracted to Zero + Maria Cornejo?

A: I'm going to be really big headed and say: intelligent, independent, free-thinking women who don't necessarily slavishly follow fashion. They buy things because they love them, because something appeals to them in a very individual way. It's more about a feeling; it's more about fitting their lifestyle. Once they start wearing the collection, they tend to get hooked.

Q: What do you think draws Michelle Obama to your clothes?

A: I think she can probably see that they flatter her shape and that they're comfortable. That's the main thing people always say—that they put them on, and they forget that they've got them on.

I think when women feel good, when they're wearing something that's comfortable, that makes them look good—they look more sensual, they have more confidence. And I think that's very empowering.

I think the whole thing is to have beautiful clothes, but to look like you just threw them on in the morning, forgot about them, and you look cool anyway. I like that.

First Debate
Oxford, MS

ATTENDING THE FIRST PRESIDENTIAL DEBATE, held at the University of Mississippi in Oxford, Mississippi, Michelle Obama returned to a favorite designer: Thakoon Panichgul. Her choice for the Friday night event, which brought together both the Democratic and Republican party presidential nominees to discuss foreign policy, was Thakoon's Inside-Out dress from the designer's Fall 2008 collection.

The sheath dress received its name for its exposed darts, in white, at the shoulders, neckline, and torso. A white band also runs vertically down each side. At first glance, the dress—with its banded ballet neck, short sleeves, and tapered hemline—may appear simplistic in cut, but its exquisite tailoring provides form-fitting sophistication for the wearer. A raised inset seam also enhances the waist. The silk radzimir fabric is a daring floral print in brown, coral pink, and yellow, with touches of cobalt blue; overlaying the floral print is a subdued latticework pattern. Mrs. Obama kept her accessories to a minimum, letting the strong design and bold pattern capture the eye. Her only embellishment was a brown satin bow pinned diagonally at the collar.

Continuing with her interest in supporting military families, Mrs. Obama invited a guest to accompany her that evening: Shannon Kendall, whose husband was completing his second tour of duty in Iraq. The two women had met at a family military roundtable event in Santa Fe, New Mexico.

SUNDAY, SEPTEMBER 28, 2008

Detroit, MI

MICHELLE OBAMA SHOWED HER POLITICAL SAVVY through her sartorial choices at a "Change We Need" campaign rally in Detroit, Michigan—one of the country's hardest-hit areas during the 2008 recession. For this downtown rally, Mrs. Obama chose wisely, wearing an off-the-rack summer dress from the Swedish company H&M. The dress cost $34.90.

Founded in Sweden, H&M is an international retailer known for its cheap-chic apparel—high fashion inspired clothes at affordable price points. Originally, the brand started in 1947 under the name Hennes, which means "hers" in Swedish. In 1968, founder Erling Persson acquired the Stockholm hunting and menswear store Mauritz Widforss and renamed his enterprise Hennes & Mauritz (H&M). Today, there are more than 1,700 H&M stores in 34 countries. Over the years, H&M has collaborated with several well-known designers to produce limited edition collections. The first such collaboration was with Karl Lagerfeld in 2004.

Mrs. Obama's dress was a timeless cotton sundress with a scoop neck, fitted waist and an A-line skirt. It sported varying horizontal stripes of black, burgundy, white, and taupe; the stripes made the dress a good antidote to summer temperatures, providing a crisp, fresh look. To accent the waist, Mrs. Obama wore one of her favorite accessories: a black patent leather belt.

"What is compelling about Mrs. Obama's style is how she wears both high fashion and low fashion–it's modern, democratic, and, above all, American."

ANDREW BOLTON, CURATOR,
THE COSTUME INSTITUTE,
THE METROPOLITAN MUSEUM OF ART

H&M sundress.

Second Debate
Nashville, TN

THE SECOND PRESIDENTIAL DEBATE, held at Belmont University in Nashville, Tennessee, was a highly anticipated event. The format was a town hall meeting and, as such, it engaged Senators Obama and McCain with the voters in a new and exciting way. More than 51 million viewers watched the debate, hosted by veteran television journalist Tom Brokaw.

Michelle Obama attended the debate, sitting next to Missouri Senator Claire McCaskill. Mrs. Obama wore a dark red, lightweight wool dress by Narciso Rodriguez. With its deep V-neckline and short sleeves, the dress had a sculptural quality to its fit; Rodriguez had applied an architect's eye toward the cut and seaming. An exposed, elongated silver zipper in the back added a fashion forward edge to the design. "I like for women to feel confident, sexy, comfortable, and completely themselves when they wear my work," said Rodriguez.

Mrs. Obama added three green diamante pins around the neckline, giving a romantic, sparkly touch to the sculptural dress. (As first lady, she would later wear two of these pins when visiting a school in Washington, D.C.) The pins, which resembled ribbon-tied bows, varied in size: the largest one was centered at the bottom of the V-neck, accenting the cut of the neckline; the two smaller pins were placed on either side, drawing attention back to Mrs. Obama's face.

WEDNESDAY, OCTOBER 15, 2008

Third Debate

Hempstead, NY

FOR THE FINAL PRESIDENTIAL DEBATE, held at Hofstra University in New York, Michelle Obama wore an iris wool crepe dress, by Maria Pinto. The cut of the bodice creates cap sleeves, which are a youthful complement to the high jewel neckline. At first glance, the dress may appear to be a simple sheath dress, but—like many of Pinto's designs—there is a nuanced approach to such seeming simplicity. Pinto apprenticed with American designer Geoffrey Beene, known as a modernist and a master technician. "Designing is an architectural problem," Beene told the *New York Times* in 1991. Pinto's training under the designer continues to show in all of her work.

Like her mentor, Pinto frequently relies on using a bias cut and princess or elliptical seaming to shape the contours of her clothes to the body. Pinto's pattern cut and seaming bring an effortless fit—and even structure—to wool crepe, a notoriously limp fabric.

To enhance her style that night, Mrs. Obama pinned three floral brooches by Erickson Beamon over a long strand of pearls. The brooches were made using vintage Bakelite and glass flowers, as part of Erickson Beamon's Victory Garden collection for Mrs. Obama. Worn as a trio, they recalled scatter pins, popular in the early 1950s. The creative use of accessories added visual interest and depth to the outfit. The feminine, even sentimental, combination of pearls and flowers was made fresh when paired with a dress of such modern, minimalist lines. Mrs. Obama completed her look with Jimmy Choo Glacier pumps in Bordeaux.

Jimmy Choo Glacier
pumps in Bordeaux.

Pittsburgh, PA

SPEAKING AT A CAMPAIGN RALLY in the Oakland neighborhood of Pittsburgh, Pennsylvania, Michelle Obama wore a dress in a decidedly autumnal palette. In a design from J.Crew's Fall 2008 collection, the dress featured a bold silk print boatneck top and slim wool flannel skirt. J.Crew named the distinctive print "Abstract rose," which consists of black brushstrokes over muted peach, deep mustard, and orange flowers.

The length of the dress was extended with a band of the same silk fabric added to the bottom hem, likely taken from a second piece purchased from J.Crew. (Mrs. Obama wore a skirt in the same material at a later date—the likely source.) Mrs. Obama, who is 5'11", is said to prefer hems that hit at the knee.

The finished look included a long, slim cardigan sweater and a large silk flower pin in a vivid shade of tangerine. The pin, made of orange silk strands that encircle a painted acrylic button, is a 1960s piece by Hattie Carnegie, secured through the Carole Tanenbaum Vintage Collection. Carole Tanenbaum is a Toronto-based, world-renowned collector of vintage costume jewelry. Her carefully curated collection includes more than 15,000 pieces, dating from the Victorian era to the 1980s. "What I love about Michelle Obama is whatever she wears, she wears—it doesn't wear her," says Tanenbaum. "It always seems to me that she has fun with what she wears. And I think that's how she makes her selections—things that charm her, colors that inspire her."

With this look, Mrs. Obama combined several of her favorite signatures: bold graphics, a floral motif, a cardigan sweater, and a large, statement brooch.

1960s era pin by Hattie Carnegie; Acquired through the Carole Tanenbaum Vintage Collection.

MONDAY, OCTOBER 27, 2008

The Tonight Show

FOR HER APPEARANCE ON *THE TONIGHT SHOW*, Michelle Obama joined host Jay Leno for a discussion about fashion, family, and the rigors of suddenly being thrust into an all-watching world. For her highly anticipated visit to the late night television show, Mrs. Obama wore a complete outfit by J.Crew. Her color palette was one of optimistic yellow, starting with the J.Crew Crystal-button colorblock cardigan in silver honey.

Underneath the cardigan, Mrs. Obama wore J.Crew's Italian Deco silk tank top, with its printed paillette pattern in bold yellow, burnt honey, and dark brown. Her skirt was J.Crew's Pembridge-dot pencil skirt in yellow gold. The sheen of the skirt fabric provided a lustrous look to the outfit and nicely balanced the cardigan, while the woven dots of the skirt fabric played off the curvy deco pattern of the top. Completing the circular motif was a large amber and silver-toned crystal brooch that pinned the cardigan top together. For shoes, Mrs. Obama wore Jimmy Choo Jade pumps in gold metallic watersnake.

When asked about the provenance of her outfit by Leno, Mrs. Obama replied, "Actually this is a J.Crew ensemble. We ladies, we know with J.Crew—you can get some good stuff online." Sharing more about her shopping habits, Mrs. Obama added, "When you don't have time, you've got to click." Mrs. Obama's choice of J.Crew attracted an influx of interested shoppers to the brand's Web site. All three of the items worn on *The Tonight Show* sold out within a matter of days.

Jenna Lyons **is a 19-year veteran of J.Crew, rising through the ranks from men's knitwear to creative director. She works from a sun-drenched office in a building high above lower Broadway, the walls decorated with a collage of tears from magazines and photographs. She is as remarkably stylish as she is down-to-earth, qualities reflected in the all-American brand that she has helped to shape.**

Q: How did you start out at J.Crew?

A: When I graduated from Parsons, I was offered a job at J.Crew in men's knits. I was so excited, I took the job without even asking the salary. It was fun for me to be able to work on clothes that most people in America could buy. I would tell someone where I worked, "J.Crew," and most people would say, "Oh yeah, I wear that brand." It's been nice to be a part of something that has changed, grown up so much, and that's so much the fabric of so many peoples' lives.

Q: What do you love about what you do?

A: Every season is new. Every season we have a different color palette, and we're looking at new inspiration. I love when the shows happen. I love poring through magazines. I love looking at prints and fabrics. I actually still really love it. It never gets old. I'm constantly excited about what's next.

Q: What was it like to see Michelle Obama wearing J.Crew on *The Tonight Show*?

A: I was watching. I remember when she came out on stage, and then when she said her outfit was J.Crew. I seriously almost took my husband's eye out. I was like, "Wake up! Wake up! Look!" I was texting [J.Crew chairman and CEO] Millard "Mickey" Drexler. The whole company was aflutter. It was hysterical. It was very exciting.

It's also nice to see your clothes worn through someone else's eyes, especially someone who puts them together beautifully. I wouldn't put that combination together, not because I don't like it, but because you do your own thing, you create things in your own way, and make them your own.

Q: Michelle Obama wore a pair of J.Crew gloves for Barack Obama's oath of office. What was your reaction?

A: We were going crazy. People were like, "Those are our gloves!" and "I touched those gloves—and now they're on the Lincoln Bible!"

Q: Thoughts on the color mix?

A: Something I've always loved about Michelle Obama's style is her sense of color—if you look at her color combinations, she figures out how to do these sort of avocado, citrus colors—she does color so well and totally understands how to do it for her skin tone. There's always a play and subtle shift in color, which is fun for us because it's sort of what we do too.

Q: What kind of response have you seen as a result of the first lady wearing J.Crew?

A: Our customers feel connected. People feel like, "Wow, she's just like me. I own something from J.Crew. I can get that catalogue, and I can get something from there too." And that is an instant connector, an instant way to say, "I'm just like you. I have to do all the things you have to do. I have to get my kids ready for school. I don't have a lot of time. I don't want to spend a million dollars." People were really touched by that, and able to relate on so many levels.

Q: What do you make of the attention on Michelle Obama's style?

A: Fashion in and of itself can feel vacant to some people. People can feel like it's something you shouldn't focus on or that it's not important. And you can debate that all day long. But I think part of the reason that people have been so focused on Michelle Obama is because she is so much more than that. And it somehow feels good to support her and to feel excited about her clothes as well, on top of that, because it's just one more way to give her accolade.

J.Crew's Italian Deco Tank, worn by Michelle Obama on *The Tonight Show*.

Election Day

Chicago, IL

ON AN UNSEASONABLY BALMY NOVEMBER MORNING, the Obamas turned casting their votes into a family affair. They arrived at their regular polling place—Shoesmith Elementary School in their Hyde Park-Kenwood neighborhood—accompanied by their two daughters. Mrs. Obama kept things simple, wearing a black scoop-neck T-shirt, black jeans, and a black cardigan sweater. She wore a black patent leather belt over the sweater. Her hair was swept back off her face with a black headband and was secured in a low ponytail. She also wore her two favorite layered necklaces: a tiny diamond peace symbol by Lena Wald and a Hope tag. The peace symbol necklace had been bought for Mrs. Obama by a friend at Trabert & Hoeffer Jewels in Chicago.

It was a look immediately recognizable to busy women everywhere: a low-key yet pulled together outfit in easy-to-wear black, plus a favorite accessory or two for a glimmer of polish and, in this case, good luck.

ABOVE: Lena Wald white gold and diamond peace sign necklace.

BELOW: Blue Moon Beads Hope charm.

Polling Place

Election Night
Chicago, IL

STARTING IN THE AFTERNOON, people began filling Grant Park for the post-election rally. Only 60,000 tickets were available to campaign workers and donors to join in the roped-off Hutchinson Field section of Grant Park, but tens of thousands more people filled in the rest of the lakefront park. Others stayed on nearby Michigan Avenue—always busy with shoppers, tourists, and urban residents—to listen to the event via loudspeakers. The night was unseasonably warm, even so close to Lake Michigan, and the mood was one of harmony, expectation, and fun.

In Grant Park, giant video screens broadcast a live news feed throughout the evening. And when the words "Breaking News" appeared on the Jumbotrons, an exuberant cheer filled the air. Next came the words "Barack Obama Elected President," and there was joyous pandemonium: shouting, hugging, jumping, and crying—all at once.

In their first appearance on election night, all four of the Obamas stepped out onto the Grant Park stage in a color-coordinated array of red and black fashion. The celebratory event was truly an occasion that warranted the coordinated effort to showcase the Obamas not merely as potential victors, but as the country's incoming first family.

Michelle Obama's dress choice—a black and red design from Narciso Rodriguez's Spring 2009 collection—was eye-catching and richly detailed. The black satin dress is sleeveless and form-fitting. A spray of red embroidery adorns the front of the dress, fading to an ombré effect. Black satin bands crisscross the waist, enhancing the hourglass figure appearance.

One of the most critically acclaimed dresses of New York Fashion Week, the dress was modified for Mrs. Obama: the neckline—a low V on the runway—was raised, and the hemline—very short and partially transparent on the runway—was lowered and lined.

ABOVE: Loree Rodkin Triple Constellation diamond earrings.

LEFT: Jimmy Choo Jade pump.

Mrs. Obama wore a cashmere cardigan by Azzedine Alaïa over the dress. For accessories, she chose Loree Rodkin's Triple Constellation earrings and diamond bangle bracelets. She also wore Jimmy Choo Jade pumps in black, which featured a low kitten heel.

Michelle Obama's style choices for the evening proved to be a harbinger of the future. While she had worn designs by Narciso Rodriguez on several high profile occasions during the campaign, she would continue—after this night—to choose Rodriguez with even more regularity once she became first lady. All of the designers Mrs. Obama wore on this most significant night were selected through the Chicago boutique Ikram.

The world didn't realize it then, but Mrs. Obama had made a major statement about her future fashion choices: she was ready to take chances with fashion-forward designers; she was ready to mix up her style; and she was dressing, ultimately, to please herself. In that regard, the evening was not just a victory celebration, but a declaration of fashion independence.

FOR THEIR FIRST PRIVATE DINNER OUT AFTER THE ELECTION, the Obamas returned to familiar territory: Spiaggia, the tony northern Italian restaurant on North Michigan Avenue in Chicago. The couple had celebrated both Valentine's Day and their wedding anniversary there in 2008.

Chicago, IL

Mrs. Obama braved the chill with a black Sonia Rykiel coat, from the French label's Fall 2008 collection. The coat has a swing cut and bracelet-length flared sleeves. (She would wear this coat again during the week of the inauguration festivities.) From underneath the jacket peeked a black pleated skirt, an Isabel Toledo design. With her hair pulled back into a chignon, Mrs. Obama accessorized with large statement earrings and a black Lanvin handbag.

The legendary Sonia Rykiel, "Queen of Knits," said of the black wool coat: "My process is a continuous story about the Rykiel woman and how she can build a wardrobe. Every season has a different theme but always works with items from previous seasons. This unique shaped coat is very cozy and easy to wear."

The Obamas entered the restaurant to the cheers of onlookers on Michigan Avenue. From the high vantage point of their table at Spiaggia, which translates to "beach" or "shore," the couple had a view of the glittering skyline of Chicago stretched out before them.

"What an inspiration to see this smart, beautiful woman who plays with color, print, and shape yet always looks appropriate for every appearance."

SONIA RYKIEL

Black wool
swing coat by
Sonia Rykiel.

White House Visit

Washington, D.C.

THE FIRST STEP IN THE TRANSITION OF POWER from George W. Bush to Barack Obama, from president 43 to incoming 44, was a White House visit between the Bushes and the Obamas. President and Mrs. Bush met the Obamas at the driveway on the South Lawn; a few moments later, the couples entered the White House. Mr. Bush gave Mr. Obama his first look at the Oval Office, while Mrs. Bush took Mrs. Obama on a tour of the first family residence on the second and third floors.

For this first meeting between the outgoing and incoming first ladies, Mrs. Obama wore a scarlet red wool crepe dress by Maria Pinto. The design is Pinto's Paulette II, with an empire waist, long sleeves and a layered, inward pleating detail at the neckline.

"What was great about that dress was that it was such a bold statement," said Cheryl Tan, former fashion writer for the *Wall Street Journal*. "The choice of that dress really said, 'I'm not a shrinking violet. I'm a dynamic person, and I'm going to be a dynamic first lady.' It sent a signal."

Wool crepe dress
by Maria Pinto.

Barbara Walters Special

IN ONE OF HER FIRST FORMAL, post-election television interviews, Mrs. Obama wore an eye-catching sleeveless dress in ivory raw silk. The sheath dress had princess seaming and black piping around its jewel neckline and armholes. At first glance, what might have appeared to be a printed fabric, was in fact the effect created by several hundred hand embroidered rosettes made of French knots. The dress was the work of Jason Wu, number 17 from his Spring 2009 collection. "I just thought it would be a nice, new way to do a print," said Jason Wu of the embroidery. "It looks like a print, and there's something geometric about it, but up close there are all of these beautiful, irregular little knots that I thought were so pretty."

The dress had been ordered from Wu by Chicago boutique owner Ikram Goldman, who had only told Wu that it was for "a special customer." The young, Taipei-born designer acknowledged to the *Wall Street Journal* blog "Heard on the Runway" that this might be a "career-launching moment" for him. His words turned out to be prophetic, for Mrs. Obama would end up wearing a Jason Wu gown for the Inaugural Ball.

At this time, Wu might not have been a household name, but he was already an established rising star in the fashion world. Having launched his first line in 2006, Wu had been named as a finalist for the 2008 CFDA/Vogue Fashion Fund prize, and his clothes were starting to appear in Neiman Marcus and smaller, cutting-edge boutiques across the country. His designs were already garnering a reputation for their exceptional finishes. For example, the hand embroidery on this dress took 100 hours of labor in Wu's New York studio.

To accent the dress, Mrs. Obama wore a black and platinum bow pin at the neckline, pinned at a jaunty angle that added a playful finishing touch.

CHAPTER V THE INAUGURATION

First Lady of Fashion

For a brief few days in January, the chill of winter seemed to subside, the worry of the mounting recession seemed to fade, and for supporters of the soon-to-be president and first lady of the United States, a spirit of celebration and new beginning took hold.

The inauguration of Barack Obama as the 44th president of the United States would be a remarkable milestone in history, celebrated through the streets of Washington and projected across all possible media around the world. Faithfully by his side throughout the experience would be the bright, poised, gracious Michelle Obama—an inspiration in her own right.

Mrs. Obama's inaugural wardrobe—a thoughtfully planned, adeptly executed mix of ensembles from her favorite American designers—would speak a language of its own. In the most authentic of ways, her clothes would range from "grown up" suits befit for her new role as first lady, to a youthful, romantic gown that channeled the fresh promise of the new administration; from a bold, graphic palette that communicated strength, to a lemongrass color that signaled an optimistic mood. Her clothes were setting the tone for the path she would carve as first lady.

The outfits chosen came from a unique range of designers, who would soon be referred to as the "New Guard" of American fashion. Though often differing in style and aesthetic, there were similarities to be found: all independent thinkers who value the craftsmanship and artistry of fashion.

The most highly anticipated ensembles were the daytime and evening looks on Inauguration Day, speculated on and prophesized by the fashion community and American public alike for weeks leading up to the inauguration. The fervor had grown so great that when President Obama introduced his wife, dressed in a white chiffon gown by Jason Wu, at the Neighborhood Ball, he would tell the crowd: "I have the special honor of being the guy who accompanied Michelle Obama to the ball."

SATURDAY, JANUARY 17, 2009

AS THE INAUGURATION NEARED, the country waited with eager anticipation for the Obamas' official arrival in Washington. More than two months had passed since the historic night in November, with the incoming first family seen only a handful of times since.

Whistle Stop Tour

Like Abraham Lincoln had a century and a half before him, Barack Obama made plans for a grand entrance into Washington—by train. The "whistle-stop" tour would depart from Philadelphia, making stops in Wilmington and Baltimore before finally arriving in Washington, D.C., that same evening.

On the morning of January 17, a crowd convened in the North Waiting Room of the 30th Street Station in Philadelphia. Mrs. Obama was smartly dressed in a tailored purple jacket and cashmere rollneck top by Zero + Maria Cornejo, paired with fitted black pants and black suede boots. She watched over her two young daughters as Barack Obama took the stage. "We are here to mark the beginning of our journey to Washington," he spoke to the crowd. "This is fitting because it was here, in this city, that our American journey began. It was here that a group of farmers and lawyers, merchants and soldiers, gathered to declare their independence and lay claim to a destiny that they were being denied."

As the train prepared to pull out of Philadelphia, the Obamas were joined by the Bidens, extended family, friends, and press—spirits high and the atmosphere festive. For outerwear, Mrs. Obama dressed in a black wool swing coat with cropped bell sleeves and an exaggerated collar by designer Sonia Rykiel. Though most of Mrs. Obama's inaugural trousseau would consist of custom pieces by American designers, this particular coat originated from the French designer's Fall 2008 collection, and had been seen once before, when Mrs. Obama joined her husband for a night out in Chicago a few days after the election. Purple leather gloves and a waffle knit scarf accented the look.

En route to Washington, the group found another reason to celebrate—Michelle Obama's 45th birthday happened to fall on the same day. As a surprise for their mom, Malia and Sasha Obama decorated the children's train car with brightly colored "Happy Birthday" banners—an iced sheet cake waiting in the wings.

After a long day, the train pulled into Washington at dusk—the Obamas had officially arrived in Washington.

Arlington National Cemetery

ON THE MORNING OF JANUARY 18, President-elect Obama and Vice President-elect Biden crossed the Potomac to visit Arlington National Cemetery. There, they paid respects at the Tomb of the Unknowns, laying a wreath at the gravesite. Michelle Obama and Jill Biden stood watching in the background, each with her right hand over her heart.

Mrs. Obama wore a custom-made, long lavender wool coat by Narciso Rodriguez, which featured distinctive inset seam detailing at the sides and waistline. Narciso Rodriguez, a designer known for his inset and cut-out detail work, said, "Because I think and design in positive and negative shapes, they [insets and cut-outs] often become part of the design or a way for me to create a shape or fit to the body." A coordinating lilac scarf and purple leather gloves kept Mrs. Obama warm in the cold January weather.

Afterward, the Obamas, joined by Michelle's mother, Marian Robinson, and daughters Malia and Sasha, attended a church service at Washington, D.C.'s 19th Street Baptist Church. Underneath her coat, Mrs. Obama wore a Narciso Rodriguez dress in plum silk and wool. She would later wear the same dress when President Obama addressed a Joint Session of Congress in February.

ROWE

"It was very clean, graphic, sophisticated— a new take on the suit."

BOOTH MOORE, *LOS ANGELES TIMES*

"We Are One" Concert

TO OFFICIALLY KICKOFF THE WEEK OF INAUGURAL CELEBRATIONS, President-elect Obama and the Inauguration Planning Committee arranged for a star-studded concert, free to the public, to be held on the steps of the Lincoln Memorial. Laura Linney and Martin Luther King III read passages by F.D.R. and John F. Kennedy, while Jamie Foxx and Steve Carell spoke of Thomas Jefferson, Thurgood Marshall, and Robert Kennedy. A range of musical performers included Bruce Springsteen, Mary J. Blige, James Taylor, Garth Brooks, Stevie Wonder, U2, Beyonce, and more. The event drew a jubilant crowd of more than 400,000 that filled the Mall.

As Mrs. Obama walked down the marble steps of the Lincoln Memorial, the world could observe a subtle shift in style that reflected her new role. Dressed in Narciso Rodriguez, as she had earlier in the day, Mrs. Obama wore an impeccably styled ensemble in camel and black. Her black top sparkled with beaded embellishment radiating from the neckline and was paired with a camel color, knee-length wool skirt, defined at the waist by a black belt.

The look was topped by a long black scarf and camel color wool coat. The coat also brought an unexpected detail—a black lining—that drew the eye in and seamlessly blended with her black top and scarf. Black leather gloves, patent leather kitten heels, and Loree Rodkin chandelier earrings, the latter borrowed from Chicago boutique Ikram, added polished touches to what was an incredibly cohesive and memorable look.

The ensemble was another high profile moment for Narciso Rodriguez. Born in New Jersey, Mr. Rodriguez became interested in fashion at an early age. "I grew up surrounded by strong Cuban women who had great personal style. Seeing what they were wearing and how the clothes moved inspired me to want to design," he said. "Rather than become an architect, which was another love of mine, I decided to incorporate architecture into fashion, which is what I do today."

At the time, Booth Moore of the *Los Angeles Times* described Michelle Obama's ensemble as, "strong, elegant and above all modern."

BATTLE BORN

FOR THE "KIDS' INAUGURAL: WE ARE THE FUTURE" CONCERT, Mrs. Obama dazzled in a blue and yellow J.Crew ensemble, a palette that reflected the bright, youthful spirit of the evening.

The night was filled with music by teen favorites Miley Cyrus, Demi Lovato,

Kids' Inaugural Concert

Bow Wow, and—to the delight of the Obama daughters—the Jonas Brothers. Mrs. Obama encouraged her young audience: "We all have something incredible to contribute to the life of this nation, and kids, this means you too, right?"

Wearing a silver-blue metallic lace shell paired with a blue wool serge pencil skirt, Mrs. Obama kept her look young and fresh by topping the ensemble with an olive-yellow cardigan; all three pieces were by J.Crew. Erickson Beamon's Techno Deco belt, a piece Mrs. Obama previously wore during the primary season, cinched her waist and added personal character. The outfit was further accessorized with a set of diamond bangle bracelets and chandelier earrings by Loree Rodkin.

The ensemble was feminine, while full of unexpected pairings. Culled from a mainstream retailer known for moderate prices, it brought a timely, achievable appeal, perfectly suited for the occasion.

Oath of Office

THRONGS OF SUPPORTERS HAD GATHERED AT THE CAPITOL FOR THE INAUGURATION, wrapped in thick winter coats and patriotic-colored scarves to brave the cold January weather. Through the sea of black outerwear, Michelle Obama shone bright, wearing a lemongrass suit by Isabel Toledo that illuminated her as a beacon of both style and optimism.

The suit consisted of a dress and coordinating coat, layered with a yellow mohair cardigan by Nina Ricci worn in between. The ensemble had a grown-up essence that felt appropriate for both the significance of the occasion and the new role Mrs. Obama was ascending to. It did, however, still offer subtle hints of the unexpected, a trademark of Mrs. Obama's style.

The suit's color, not quite yellow, not quite green, was aptly described as "lemongrass" by designer Isabel Toledo. "I wanted to pick a very optimistic color, that had sunshine," Toledo told the *New York Times*. "I wanted her to feel charmed, and in that way would charm everybody." The appearance of the fabric, too, was quite changeable, as the layered Swiss wool lace, backed with tulle netting and lined in white silk taffeta, took on a subtle shimmer at times.

The choice of designer, Isabel Toledo, a Cuban-American celebrated within the inner circles of fashion, but not widely known to the American public, was in itself significant. The choice signaled a recognition of one of American fashion's greatest talents, one known for her old-world, hand craftsmanship.

Describing her design process for the ensemble, Ms. Toledo said, "I saw the fabric, and said, 'That's it!' I knew I could make her luminous. The light was going to come from within." The texture of the fabric, in particular, was significant: "To me, that moment had to have more than one dimension. I knew I could create depth with the lace."

Mrs. Obama paired the ensemble with grass green J.Crew leather gloves and green Jimmy Choo Glacier pumps that offered a fresh play on color. A Victorian rhinestone sash pin from the Carole Tanenbaum Vintage Collection was worn at the neckline, bringing light and sparkle to Mrs. Obama's face.

The newly appointed first lady was not the only budding style icon of the morning. Malia and Sasha Obama both wore brightly colored coats from Crew Cuts by J.Crew.

Designer Isabel Toledo added a tie closure to the lemongrass lace coat for light movement.

Isabel Toledo learned to sew from a babysitter at the age of eight. With her parents and two sisters, she emigrated from Cuba, making a new home in West New York, New Jersey. When their mother had to go to work, the girls resisted a babysitter, but were more open to "sewing classes." It was there that Ms. Toledo first discovered her love of the craft. She has been designing for the past 25 years, with a unique process that is both intimate and personal. It was no surprise, then, that her lemongrass dress and coat worn by Michelle Obama for Inauguration Day brought tremendous meaning and substance.

Q: It's been reported that you grew up sewing from a very early age and began by customizing your hand-me-downs. Do you remember your first original design?

A: I do! The most important thing about my first design was what I managed to do without. I made a design with no industrial closure. No zipper, no buttons or button fly. The sophistication of those finishes were way beyond my years. It was a pair of pants with extensions that wrapped around the body to keep them closed. I was very proud of my achievement.

Q: What about you as a designer is the same now as it was then?

A: To this day, ingenuity supersedes my thirst of fashion, I still LOVE a smart pattern.

Q: And what's different?

A: My appreciation for the complex ritual of tradition.

Q: How do you want a woman to feel in your clothes?

A: Dressing is an act of communication. Being in control of the message is key to feeling confident. My service is to provide designs to accommodate different moods—the most important of those— to be in LOVE with yourself and the world.

Q: What, for you, is the magic in opposites? What are your favorite opposites?

A: Opposites create balance. My favorites: Ruben and Isabel, hard and soft, day and night, the intimate and the public.

Q: Will you describe how you developed the lemongrass suit Mrs. Obama wore for the inauguration?

A: The truth is, I took a creative mini-tantrum. I felt the importance of the moment and really wanted to address the personal, historical, and spiritual significance.

Q: Was it a collaborative process with Mr. Ruben Toledo [Isabel's husband, an acclaimed fashion illustrator]?

A: I'll say: As I was pacing back and forth, verbalizing the importance of the swearing in moment, for me and for the world . . . after much philosophizing, Ruben turned (probably with impatience, and a pencil and paper) and said, "Well what do you want it to look like?" I reached out for the swatch of fabric that had fueled my tantrum for creative discovery and began to formulate the vision that became the "lemongrass" look. This textile held the key.

Q: How did you want the first lady to feel while wearing it?

A: The joy of accomplishment, the optimism of our country's future. I wanted her to feel the labor of love that went into making it.

Q: Why did you choose the lemongrass color? And what did you want it to communicate?

A: The color evoked warmth, a pacific and calming emotion. I don't know why; it just symbolized a new day.

Q: The fabric also had notable depth and texture—what was the significance of the fabric?

A: The personal significance is my love of lace. It is at once fragile and incredibly strong. It gives me an opportunity to say more because you can create depth with the layers. In this case, the immediate layer was the lightest of silk tulle combined with the pop white of the silk taffeta.

Q: Is there a reason you wanted the coat to tie closed, rather than button?

A: Michelle is a woman with a great American stride. I cannot imagine her being restricted by clothes. One button, one tie, in fact it had both, just not visible. The placement was what was most important, near her heart. This proportion

Designer Isabel Toledo sits for a portrait by her husband Ruben.

for the opening gives length and grace to her walk, and the tie added a light movement. It was important she feel the freedom to walk down Pennsylvania Ave.

Q: What was your reaction when you learned the first lady had chosen your ensemble? What was the spirit around your atelier?
A: You can imagine, we were all in a supreme state of HAPPINESS! We all saw it for the first time on television along with the rest of the world. The impact of that moment was a universal HIGH. We were charmed by the vision of our new first lady looking so regal and radiant, and then it hit us that it was our "lemongrass" coat and dress she was wearing. After that we all cried, hugged, cheered, were glued to the television in Ruben's painting studio until the moment Barack Obama with Michelle at his side was sworn in. Then it was a total New Year's celebration not only in our studio but in the entire neighborhood. I have left in my heart a special place for my creative tantrum. I call it a job well done.

Q: What do you enjoy most about what you do?
A: The selfishness of creation, the satisfaction of problem solving, the joy of discovery.

Q: What are the advantages of running a smaller, independent atelier?
A: The advantages are that we have healthy limitations. Therefore, we employ "necessity," the mother of invention. My small staff and I get to work on all the clothes we make. We get to invest time and energy on perfecting the craft we all love. This is a very satisfying way to evolve my business. The LOVE of MAKE is in every one of the garments with an ISABEL TOLEDO label.

Q: Do you have a favorite dress?
A: My favorite dress is yet to be created. I'll let you know in the future.

TOLEDO
FABRICACION
EXCLUSIVA
Jersey
"SIDE SADDLE SUIT"

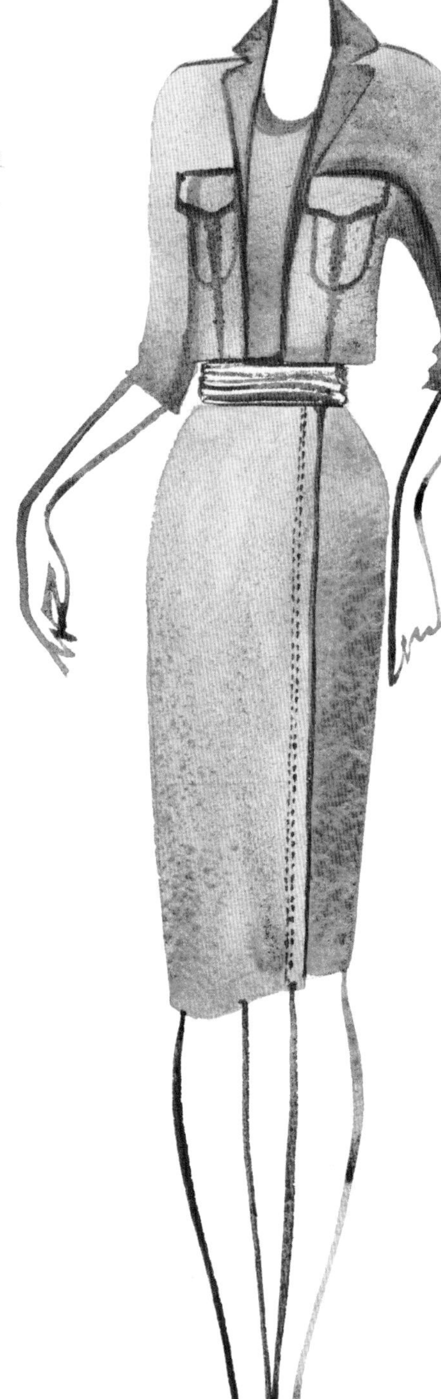

Designs by Isabel Toledo for First Lady Michelle Obama. Illustrations by Ruben Toledo.

Colour # 22
Colour # 4
TOLEDO
FABRICACION
EXCLUSIVA
Wool Jersey

Inaugural Ball

AFTER MONTHS OF SPECULATION AND HUNDREDS OF DESIGNS, the world was finally treated to Michelle Obama's Inaugural Ball gown—a gown for the ages.

As the president and first lady took the dance floor at the Neighborhood Ball, serenaded by Beyonce Knowles's rendition of the Etta James classic "At Last," First Lady Michelle Obama dazzled in her ivory chiffon, one-shoulder gown embellished with organza flowers and crystals.

The designer of Mrs. Obama's gown was Jason Wu, then only 26 years old. Wu's name officially entered the Inaugural Ball gown race after he dressed Mrs. Obama for a television interview with Barbara Walters in late November. Still, as late as a December interview with the *Wall Street Journal*'s "Heard on the Runway" blog, Wu downplayed the possibility of designing the Inaugural Ball gown, saying, "Oh, that's a long shot!"

Describing his inspiration for the dress, Jason Wu later told CNN, "It's about hope. It's about newness," he said. "It's all a little dreamlike, and we're making history, and I wanted to really reflect that."

The gown had a youthful and romantic spirit that reflected a different facet of the first lady's style, almost in contrast to the grown-up suit she had worn earlier in the day. On the evening of January 20, 2009, there was no question—Michelle Obama was the belle of the ball.

The dress was complemented by a suite of custom-designed jewelry by Loree Rodkin that included 61-carat diamond Inaugural earrings, the 13-carat Michelle signet ring, and a set of white gold bangles featuring 13 carats of diamonds.

To coordinate with her gown, the First Lady wore a pair of white Satin d'Orsay sandals by Jimmy Choo; Tamara Mellon, founder and president of Jimmy Choo, described the choice as, "the perfect finishing touch for her Jason Wu evening dress." An ivory, cropped dress jacket by Jason Wu topped the ensemble.

Loree Rodkin **has lived a fascinating life. She is a former talent manager turned jewelry designer, who grew up in Chicago and spent her first trip to Paris in the company of Salvador Dalí. She has designed jewelry for a host of celebrity clientele—from Madonna to Mary J. Blige, Cher to Aerosmith. Her jewelry combines modern and medieval, with a clear Gothic influence. It's not a combination that one might expect to appeal to the first lady—which makes it all the more exciting that indeed, it does.**

Q: How did your interest in jewelry design begin? How did it evolve into a business?

A: When I was 12, my mother began to give me jewelry for my birthday every year, and I hated it, always. She was so fed up with buying me stuff I didn't like, that she gave me access to the family jeweler and said I could make my own jewelry. And that's really how it started. It was a little hobby of mine. Later when I was managing actors, Robert Downey Jr. and Brad Pitt, it's what I did to stay sane. My line was launched in 1989 at Maxfield in LA.

Q: Your designs have a distinct aesthetic. What attracts you to Gothic architecture and imagery?

A: I think the ornate-ness, the richly embellished aspects of that period of architecture. There was great dimension and attention to detail. And the shapes and imagery—I think there was something dark and romantic about the Gothic period.

Q: One of the first times Michelle Obama wore your earrings was on election night. Were you aware that she owned them and was planning to wear them?

A: I had no idea. I was watching along with the rest of the country and was like, "Wow, those look just like my earrings." But you know, I couldn't even wrap my head around the fact that my earrings were on her. It's kind of like, "Oh gosh, those are so similar to mine," and then, "Oh, those *are* mine!"

Q: What inspired those earrings?

A: They were the Constellation earrings. I really wanted something with movement. I draw inspiration from so many things. Nature, architecture, fabrics, a mood. The shapes were a reference to the planets and the galaxies and how they revolve around each other. I'm always mixing shapes and forms. In Gothic architecture there's lots of layering and texturing.

Q: For the inauguration, I've read you were commissioned to create several suites of jewelry. Did you receive a brief?

A: Ikram [Goldman] requested that I submit four suites of jewelry. I was asked to design pieces with no color—so white diamonds. But otherwise, it was really free range. I knew Mrs. Obama had a long neck, so I took into account how long I wanted the earrings to be. And I wanted a piece that was like a signet ring, that felt like a White House Oval Office moment, with a twist.

Q: What does it mean to you as a designer that the first lady of the United States wears your jewelry?

A: It's like winning an Academy Award. It's such an honor.

Q: Did you ever dream your pieces would end up in the Smithsonian?

A: I don't think anyone dreams that big. It's amazing. It's hard to imagine that this could have happened. When Ikram called and said, "We'd like to do some stuff for the inauguration," I said, "Are you sure you dialed the right one?"

Q: What do you think attracts Mrs. Obama to your jewelry?

A: I think there's a uniqueness to my jewelry. It doesn't look like anything else anyone else is designing. And I think she is fashion forward and has a great, strong point of view when it comes to fashion and herself, so I think that appealed to her. And Ikram is a big champion of mine. She was one of the first people to ever carry my jewelry. So I would say, really, Ikram is responsible.

Q: What do you love about designing jewelry?

A: I love getting to create, to imagine something and give it life. Plus I'm a girl—we love shiny, sparkly things.

3R

Jason Wu has talent and recognition that far surpass his young years. He designs for a modern woman, with a quality ethic and old-world craftsmanship that hearken back to another time. Of Chinese descent, Jason Wu was born in Taipei, Taiwan. At age nine, he moved with his family to Vancouver, British Columbia, where he learned English, discovered *Vogue* and first learned to sew. He later attended fashion school at Parsons in New York, interned at Narciso Rodriguez, and in 2008, was a finalist for the *Vogue* / CFDA Fashion Fund prize. When Michelle Obama began to wear his designs, there was no question—American fashion had found its future.

Q: How and when did you start designing?

A: My mother bought me a sewing lesson when I was 11. I didn't have a dress form or a work room. I used dolls as mannequins. My mom found a fashion student through the local community college to come in and teach me to sew once a week. That's how I learned techniques and how to use a sewing machine.

My parents were a little more forward thinking. My mom sort of carved out my future for me, not by saying, "This is what you're going to do," but by putting me in the right environments where I could discover what I wanted to do.

By 15 or 16, I decided being a fashion designer was it. I was 16 when I started to design for dolls. I was in boarding school for a long time, and I was dying to do something. I found this job to design for dolls on the side, outside of school, and it became a thing on its own.

Q: Is there anything from designing for dolls that has stayed with you?

A: It's very different—but the attention to detail. Once you've seen something in a miniature scale, you really pay attention to every loose thread. I'm the person that before a show, I'm clipping a loose thread on a model. Though no one will see it, I'm aware of those things. That's from working in small scale.

Q: Have you always had a vision of the kind of clothes you wanted to make?

A: I didn't set out to say, "This is who I am." I'm still discovering that. Season by season, we're still learning. But I came out with a very specific aesthetic that was always me, something I liked, and, I never saw my woman being anything else.

Q: Will you describe this aesthetic?

A: It's detail oriented, it's investment dressing, there's a timeless element—but it's youthful. We go on trunk shows, and we can dress a woman who's in her 40s, and we can dress a woman in her 20s. It's a piece that can withstand the test of time. There's detail and quality that I always thought was missing in a lot of today's clothes. I always felt that old-world couture was so well made, inside and out. Those elements are so great and I wanted to bring that to my work, but do it in a very youthful and modern way.

Q: So for you, craftsmanship and attention to detail are clearly important.

A: I think they're the most important. You have to see and feel the difference. I think those are important aspects to designer clothes. I think that's what defines luxury.

Luxury has become something of a diluted term in the last ten years. We had so much of everything. We did have a lot, come to think of it. At one point people could charge so much money for things that weren't worth that much, and people would believe it because it was "designer," because it was "luxury." But what was really luxury? People are forced to think about it now. Is luxury something that's just really expensive? Or something that holds its value and is worth the price?

Q: For the Inaugural Ball gown, we read Ikram relayed, "it had to sparkle." From there, how did the dress develop?

A: I had a vision. I said, "This is going to be a white dress, we're going to do that." And that's what I sent. I sent a sketch with a swatch with the embroidery. Ikram said, "Make it."

We made the fabric. That's one thing most people don't see on the screen. It's so white that you don't see it. It was really intricate. At one point we were all sitting around the table sewing on the flowers. The whole team was sewing. This had to be one of a kind—so that it was. I really didn't know it was going to become the Inaugural Ball dress. It was a gown, so I thought it might be.

Q: What was your reaction when you saw the first lady in your gown?

A: I cried my eyes out for an hour. I really did. That was such a moment. It was a moment, and the whole world saw it. And it was a moment because I never expected it. My mom called me in five minutes—from Taiwan—and said, "Oh my God, that is *your* dress." She hadn't known I was making the dress at all. They announced it in Taiwan. It was incredible.

Q: What impact has this experience had?

A: One thing that has changed: up until last year, my extended family had not so much of an idea of what I was doing. But now, in Taiwan, this has become important news. There's never been a Taiwanese designer that has done this sort of a thing. It has made people re-think the way the art is perceived. I think that's the most important aspect. It may open doors. Things have changed a lot over the past few years, but I think this has definitely helped. It may pave the road for people who may not have had the opportunity to pursue this sort of career.

WEDNESDAY, JANUARY 21, 2009

National Prayer Service

ON HER FIRST FULL DAY AS FIRST LADY, Mrs. Obama joined her husband and the Bidens to attend a multi-denominational service at Washington National Cathedral. Mrs. Obama wore a bold print dress by Tracy Feith. With a rounded neck, fitted bodice, cummerbund waist, and full skirt, the dress offered a modern twist on a classic 1950s silhouette. The cotton dress fabric, a repeated print of cranes in patches of wisteria, was developed by Kona Bay, a Hawaii-based fabric company.

"It was a real thrill for our 'little-engine-that-could' company to see the first lady in Tracy's dress and to receive such quick recognition," Tracy Feith's partner, Susan Winget, told *Grazia Daily*. "We are beyond flattered." In the same article, Mr. Feith observed, "[Michelle Obama] likes things that are feminine but somewhat adventurous. She's not afraid of those things. She's not letting people just make suggestions."

The same day, the Obamas hosted an open house at the White House, welcoming people who had volunteered for the campaign, and others who had simply waited at the White House gates with the hopes of getting in. It was a gesture that signaled the openness and inclusiveness the Obamas would bring to their new home.

Kona Bay Fabrics, Emperor Collection II, repeated print of cranes in patches of wisteria.

CHAPTER VI THE WHITE HOUSE

Style and Substance in the White House

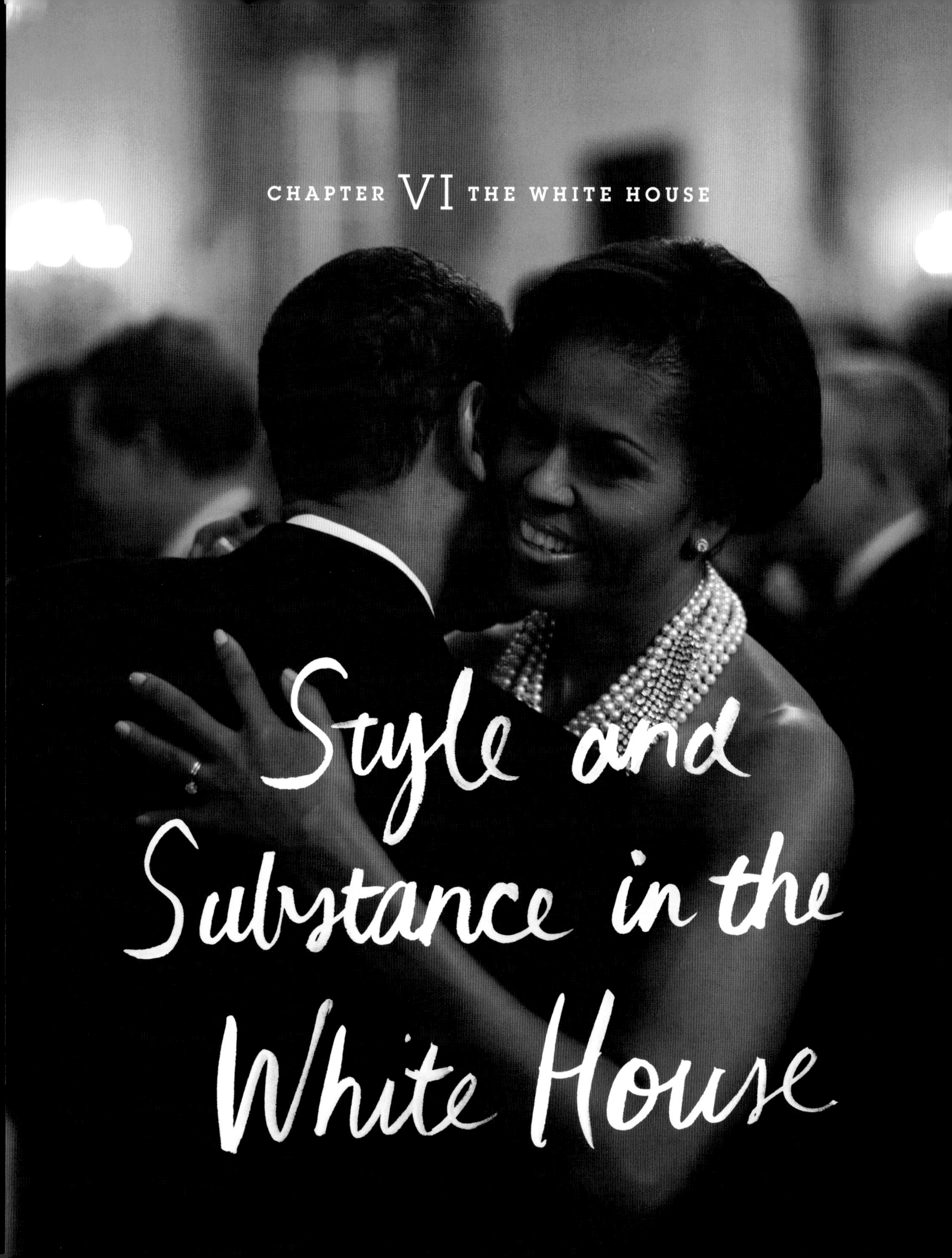

While it was unknown how Michelle Obama would embrace her new role as first lady, it was almost certain that she would forge her own unique path. Throughout 2009, the country would see the self-titled "Mom-in-chief" champion a number of social issues—national service, healthy eating, and support for military families—all the while hosting high-profile functions at the White House, soaking in Washington, D.C. culture, and most importantly, caring for her family. She was exemplary of yet another issue she had long championed: helping women to achieve work and family balance.

As Michelle Obama's influence as first lady grew, so too, did that of her wardrobe—making headlines, shaping retail trends and inspiring women everywhere. For a March 2009 feature interview in *Vogue*, Michelle Obama told editor-at-large André Leon Talley: "I love clothes. First and foremost, I wear what I love. That's what women have to focus on: what makes them happy and what makes them feel comfortable and beautiful. If I can have any impact, I want women to feel good about themselves and have fun with fashion."

In her first months in the White House, Mrs. Obama's White House style continued to evolve, including an expanded, eclectic range of designers. Adding further variety, Mrs. Obama's ensembles reflected the diverse roles she had taken on—from glamorous hostess to accomplished speaker to budding gardener. "Michelle, for a lot of us, represents new," said Joe Zee, creative director for *Elle* magazine. "A new president, a new era, a new look. You can't help but embrace the change and energy she has immediately brought to the capital."

While the clothes told their own captivating story, the intrigue was genuinely the total woman—a first lady of both great style and substance. Her spirit is summed up by the legendary Diane von Furstenberg: "Michelle Obama represents the modern, confident, intelligent woman. Her personality will have a huge effect on fashion."

TRADITIONALLY, one of the first tasks completed in a new administration is the unveiling of the official portrait of the first lady. Its importance is largely symbolic, as an illustrative harbinger of things to come; it defines the first lady, and it sets a public tone for the private side of the incoming administration.

First Lady Official Portrait

In her official portrait, Michelle Obama stands in the Blue Room of the White House, facing the camera straight on. Her posture, along with her full smile, conveys an openness and accessibility. She wears a black crepe jersey dress, featuring a racer-back cut, by Michael Kors. The dress originated from the designer's Spring 2009 collection. "Sportswear has never entered the White House before," said Michael Kors. "Wearing a dress with an athletic inspiration? That's new."

Though this was one of the first times Mrs. Obama had chosen Michael Kors for a high-profile event, it would certainly not be the last. Mr. Kors is known for designs that exemplify American, self-possessed chic, executing basics with such care and in luxury fabrics that they immediately become classics—an aesthetic that Mrs. Obama would increasingly embrace.

Mrs. Obama accessorized the gown with a double strand of pearls and Cartier's Tank Francaise watch in steel. The Cartier Tank watch, designed by a company steeped in French heritage and manufactured in Switzerland, has interesting ties to the United States. Designed in 1917, the first model was presented to General Pershing when he was in Paris after WWI. The shape and name is a reference to the American tanks sent to the battlefields of Europe during the war. Pierre Rainero, style and heritage director for Cartier says, "There was already a link in the birth of the watch with America," adding, "We are very honored that Mrs. Obama has chosen that watch. It's such a symbol of elegance and modernity."

Cartier Tank Francaise steel watch.

Michael Kors has built one of the most successful brands in fashion over the past 30 years, with classic, all-American sportswear at its core. While the first lady tends to favor smaller ateliers, she has worn Michael Kors designs on multiple occasions, including one that will surely become iconic—her official portrait.

Q: As a young man, do you remember style being something you associated with a first lady?

A: Certainly. For me, the overriding visual theme has always been Jackie Kennedy, in all of her different incarnations. She made the best choices in each decade, and it was always her point of view, filtered through whatever was happening in the decade: short and chic and Givenchy-like in the White House, even if Oleg Cassini was making it; in the '70s it was her own working girl version of Faye Dunaway in "Network"; and in the '80s she became a majestic grand dame. It was always done with simplicity.

Q: Your line celebrates classic Americana fashion. Will Michelle Obama become one of the people you think about while you're still planning a collection?

A: The way I design, it's like a crazy Fellni movie in my brain, like in *8 1/2* with all these memories of different women. I tap into storage of memories of women who are friends, who are clients, women who I've never met. Anyone from an assistant to a friend to the first lady to Doris Duke—it's a porridge of all these women. Yes, now Mrs. Obama has entered my lexicon. But I don't ever design a certain dress for a certain woman. It's a variety, a group of women that I'm turned on by. And it seems they're turned on by what we do too.

Q: First Lady Michelle Obama wore your dress for her official portrait. How did you find out, and what was your reaction?

A: I had no idea that was going to happen! I was in London, in the theater, and at intermission my BlackBerry went berserk—like 200 e-mails. Immediately I felt very proud and excited. My first thoughts were on the word elegant. When you hear that word now it can seem so old-fashioned. Let's be honest, life now is not exactly carefree and elegant. So it can be tricky to look elegant in this day and age. But when I saw that picture, I thought she was the picture of elegance. I thought she looked timeless and timely. I was excited about how well the dress looked, and I also thought she looked really comfortable.

Q: What influence do you think—or hope—Michelle Obama will have on American fashion?

A: Number one, I think the biggest thing is that she's busy. She's probably busier than we could imagine. She has kids, she's traveling, she's the first lady—yet she still enjoys getting dressed and looking great. So she's sending out this message that enjoying fashion and looking good doesn't exclude educated women. She gives off the message that it's okay to be interested in fashion and taken seriously. But at the same time, I think she's showing people that you can mix your clothes up, you don't have to be so rigid in how you get dressed—you can take the same belt and wear it five different ways, five different times.

And I think that she has so many price points in her closet—that's how modern people dress. That's exciting and very different. Quite frankly, we haven't had anyone in the White House like this before.

Q: What do you love most about what you do?

A: I love seeing the transformation. I love to see everything come together. It's like when an orchestra hits a chord. . . . The right clothes, accessorized the right way, on the right person. Fashion is something that never stands still. And I like the idea that there's always something new. You think you've solved the puzzle, but suddenly it changes. I love the idea of change.

Q: Change? That's something the Obama's know about.

A: Exactly. It works in fashion and works in politics.

Speaking at the Time 100 Gala in New York, Michelle Obama wore a square neck tank gown by Michael Kors, paired with a custom corset belt by Peter Soronen, and jewelry by Loree Rodkin.

ON A BRISK WINTER DAY, First Lady Michelle Obama lunched with Washington, D.C., mayor Adrian Fenty, his wife Michelle, and Jill Biden at Georgia Brown's, a District restaurant known for its traditional Southern cuisine.

Mrs. Obama dressed in a colorful medley of blues. Her dress, Maria Pinto's Ella design, was made of Prussian blue cashmere, and paired with a blue-green cardigan and a royal blue patent leather belt. For shoes, Mrs. Obama wore her bottle green Jimmy Choo Glacier pumps from the inauguration.

Her blue tweed overcoat was a J.Crew design, made with an oversize face-framing portrait collar. The asymmetric cut of the dress underneath added an edgy, modern twist to the ensemble. And the mix of colors—from bottle green to Prussian blue to blue-green—infused the outfit with a youthful, spontaneous brand of glamour.

Kennedy Center Performance

PRESIDENT AND MRS. OBAMA, accompanied by their daughters, attended a special program at the Kennedy Center: the golden anniversary show of the Alvin Ailey American Dance Theater. The troupe is known for merging African American cultural expression with the American modern dance tradition. Photographers were allowed to snap pictures as the Obamas were ushered into a red VIP box decorated with the presidential seal.

Mrs. Obama wore a striking two-tone dress by Scottish designer Jonathan Saunders. Owing to a clever construction, at first glance the dress appeared to be a metallic sheath partially covered by one of Mrs. Obama's signature cardigans. The matte material created an illusion of a separate garment; it also enhanced the sleek fit of the dress with a slimming effect. A Moschino brooch, made of metallic beads and tulle, finished the look.

Jonathan Saunders, a Scottish-born designer, graduated from the Glasgow School of Art in 1999 with a BA in printed textile. From there, he attended Central Saint Martins in London, where he graduated with a master's degree in 2002. Along with designing for his own label, he frequently consults on the creation of prints for some of the largest fashion houses in Europe. He brings a labor-intensive process to his use of traditional silk-screening methods, sometimes using up to 20 screens per design. In 2003, Saunders was commissioned by Alexander McQueen to create a series of printed textiles, which became McQueen's celebrated bird-of-paradise prints.

In his most recent collections, Saunders has demonstrated his range as a designer, showcasing expertise in clean lines, paneling and piecing, evidenced by Mrs. Obama's dress from his Fall 2008 collection.

> "When you look back through history at Jackie Kennedy or Frances Cleveland, those were moments when we could feel like we were chic Americans. Michelle Obama is really making us feel like chic Americans again."
>
> **BOOTH MOORE**, *LOS ANGELES TIMES*

SEAL OF THE PRESIDENT OF THE UNITED STATES

PRESIDENT AND MRS. OBAMA ATTENDED THE REOPENING OF FORD'S THEATRE, the site of Abraham Lincoln's assassination in 1865. The theater had undergone a $25 million, 18-month renovation, and its reopening ceremony was held on the eve of the 16th president's 200th birthday. Those in the audience stood and turned to applaud the Obamas as they made their way down the center aisle to "Hail to the Chief." The president spoke of "honoring the hallowed space" and of how Lincoln's passion for education and the arts will thrive at the famous building. Actors and artists performed, including violinist Joshua Bell, who opened the show with a traditional spiritual that hadn't been played since the night Lincoln was shot.

In honor of Lincoln's bicentennial, Mrs. Obama wore a festive dress by Isabel Toledo. Its feminine silhouette, created by a banded empire waist and a full skirt (worn with a petticoat underneath), was accented as Mrs. Obama moved across the stage. The dress was an older, existing piece by Isabel Toledo that the designer didn't know Mrs. Obama owned; it had been purchased through Ikram in Chicago at an earlier date. The fabric is an embroidered plaid on black net, with diagonal lines of bronze material that cross the skirt. As an accessory, Mrs. Obama chose her diamond bangles by Loree Rodkin.

Department of Transportation

ON A TOUR OF FEDERAL AGENCIES, Mrs. Obama spoke to the employees at the Department of Transportation. She wore a large-scale brown and black houndstooth check bolero jacket over a black turtleneck with trousers. The jacket is by Peter Soronen, from his Fall 2008 collection. The short length of the jacket is beautifully balanced by its long, tight sleeves. On her lapel, Mrs. Obama pinned the same brooch she wore to see the Alvin Ailey American Dance Theater at the Kennedy Center: a cluster of metallic beads backed by a circle of silk tulle. The brooch, from Moschino's Spring 2009 collection, brings an unexpected pop of pattern and texture to the jacket. And its oversize scale is perfectly in proportion with the check of the jacket. Mrs. Obama wore her hair up in a low twist, so the details of the jacket collar and the pin were highlighted.

Speaking to the Transportation employees, Mrs. Obama said, "As you have heard, I have taken on what I think is the fun task of coming to every department in Washington—because I want to meet my new neighbors, learn more about the community, get to know our coworkers and meet everyone who's going to be standing side by side with us over this wonderful journey that we're on," she said.

"But it's important as a reminder to let people know that the nation's business is carried out by all of you, dedicated public servants like the folks standing behind me, all of you here, who have devoted their careers, who have been doing this work for decades. So my job is simple: I'm here to say thank you. Thank you."

LEFT: Metallic beads and silk tulle brooch by Moschino.

ABOVE: Cropped houndstooth jacket by Peter Soronen.

SHORTLY BEFORE HOSTING HER FIRST BLACK-TIE DINNER, Mrs. Obama welcomed six culinary students from L'Academie de Cuisine, in nearby Gaithersburg, Maryland, to the White House kitchen to preview the menu. "This is where the magic happens," she said, introducing them to White House chef Cristeta Comerford and pastry chef Bill Yosses, who offered the students a private tasting of the upcoming dinner.

Mrs. Obama wore a cocktail-length dress by Jason Wu, similar in style to the dress she had worn for a television interview with Barbara Walters in November 2008. The violet dress, from Wu's Spring 2009 collection, is sleeveless and fitted through the bodice. A narrow panel of the dress material runs down the center from the neckline, with gathering detail on either side. Hand-embroidered black knots dot the entire dress.

"The way I do embellishment isn't with big stones. It's always about subtle elegance. This could be a day dress, but the amount of work is certainly equivalent to an evening dress—the way it's finished, inside with the contrast binding and so clean on the back."

Violet cocktail dress with French knot embroidery by Jason Wu.

SUNDAY, FEBRUARY 22, 2009

FOR THE BLACK-TIE DINNER WELCOMING THE NATIONAL GOVERNORS ASSOCIATION, Michelle Obama changed from her Jason Wu dress (worn during the visit of the culinary students) to a stunning strapless evening gown by Peter Soronen. The Twilight gown, from Soronen's Fall 2008 collection, features one of his signature corset tops and a long bias-cut skirt with flowing movement. The entire dress was covered in sequins on chiffon. While the color of the gown was a mix of deep purple and ink blue, its hue was changing and elusive, remaining true to its twilight name.

2009 Governors' Dinner

Balancing the strapless gown was a statement necklace by Tom Binns. This dramatic piece of jewelry consisted of multi-strands of pearls overlaying a bib necklace of rhinestones. The rhinestone section of the necklace was designed in squares that lay flat against the body, while the pearl strands were exuberantly looped into overlapping circles. The necklace was from Binns's Pearls in Peril collection.

RIGHT:
Sequin fabric in deep purple and ink blue, used for Peter Soronen's Twilight gown.

Peter Soronen **designs offer beautifully crafted shape and structure, often infused with his trademark corsetry. They are qualities that suit the kind of women he likes to design for: "A woman who's strong, who likes a garment that's well built, who understands her clothes." A native of Michigan, he was discovered by Joan Weinstein of Chicago in the mid-1990s, and now runs his business from New York. Michelle Obama wore his designs on the campaign trail, and has dazzled in his formal gowns at the White House.**

Q: How did your career as a designer begin?

A: I grew up outside of Detroit, in Farmington Hills. I was working in a salon; one thing led to another, and I started to make clothes for the girls there. As I got a little better at it, I took night classes for pattern making, and then in 1990, I went to Chicago for fashion school.

In 1995, a friend of mine cold-called Ultimo [in Chicago], told them that she was my representative, and said, "I would like to bring Peter in so that you can look at his clothes." She made an appointment for me in one week's time. I only had five days. I was so upset. Of course you're never ready, you never have enough money, you never have all of that.

When I got there, the buyer just flipped right through all of my daywear and stopped when she got to the evening wear. She said, "What's this?" They ordered several of the dresses and they sold them! And that started my relationship with Ultimo and Joan Weinstein. That was the first store I was carried in. I still have that first order of Joan Weinstein's writing—she has such a beautiful cursive writing. It was such a thrill of a cab ride back to my studio.

Later, I remember asking Joan if I could move to New York, and she said, "I think that would be a very good idea." So, with $5 in my pocket and a bolt of fabric, I found a studio in the Garment District. And I actually lived and worked there. I was an urban pioneer. I had to build out the bathroom, and hide that I was living there from the landlord!

Q: How did your clothes end up being carried at Ikram?

A: There was a change of hands at Ultimo. Joan had left, and they were doing something different. Ikram [who had been at Ultimo with Weinstein] picked up where they left off. By that time, I had moved to New York. Ikram called me and said, "I'm coming to see your clothes—tomorrow." The next thing I knew, she was knocking on my little studio door on the 13th floor. She began carrying my clothes during her first or second season in business.

Q: Corsetry has, from very early on, been a defining characteristic of your designs. What attracts you to it? What first triggered the interest?

A: I had an interest in watching old black-and-white movies and the spare-no-expense costumes that they would do. There would be scenes where women would put on corsets and then their dresses, and I was just so fascinated by what that would really do for them. It just looked so mature and elegant and regal. I just had to know how to do it.

I started constructing from books basically, and these old patterns from the Victorian age. As I got more clever with corsetry, I adapted it to a more modern shape and woman, and then incorporated it into dresses finally, which was really just the foundation. Without that, it didn't seem like there was any kind of dress. It just stuck with me. And I couldn't do anything without putting a lot of guts into it—the steel bones.

Q: Do you have a favorite dress that Michelle Obama has worn?

A: My favorite is probably one that you haven't seen yet—the red dress. But by far, from what has been seen, the Twilight gown was one of my favorite pieces in the Fall '08 collection. For her to be able to wear that was just fantastic.

I don't remember in my lifetime seeing a First Lady look like that. She looked glamorous! I think that helps a lot of people become more aware of what fashion can be, but I think it helps fashion too, as far as fashion houses go. I think it just reemphasizes that looking good is something. Whereas T-shirts and sweatshirts have been such the rule for so long, I'm glad there's an interest in nice things again.

Q: Are there specific inspirations behind your collections?

A: Once we get fabrics together, that's where I start to put together a story. And then an organic process begins to shift the fabric into a dress, what length it should be, short or full. The fabric dictates what I imagine it should be.

I go to fabric showrooms, I pick what my eye likes. I actually picture the whole dress, right then and there. Whether or not that develops into anything, I don't know. When I saw this fabric, for example, I saw the dress in my head [referring to sequined chiffon used for the Twilight gown]. I kind of know immediately what I want to do with the fabric. Fabric always does what it wants to do, and you never try to fight it.

Q: What do you love about being a designer?

A: The reaction a client has when she's wearing my clothes for the first time. That is such a thrill and it never goes away. It's always exciting, because it's exciting for them. To be able to take this one or two dimensional thing and then put it through a sewing machine with your hands, to be able to create something that someone's going to rock—that's the thrill of being a designer.

Peter Soronen corset gown—the red dress—worn for the Alfalfa Club Dinner in January 2009. Media was not permitted at the event, but this photo was released by the White House at a later date.

TUESDAY, FEBRUARY 24, 2009

Address to Congress

WHEN PRESIDENT OBAMA DELIVERED HIS FIRST SPEECH TO A JOINT SESSION OF CONGRESS, First Lady Michelle Obama watched from her mezzanine level box in the House of Representatives. She was joined by several special guests for the evening, including Ty'Sheoma Bethea, a student at J.V. Martin Junior High School in Dillon, South Carolina. Ms. Bethea had written a letter to Congress imploring them to help her deteriorating, partially condemned school building.

President Obama read a portion of Ms. Bethea's letter during his speech:

"We are just students trying to become lawyers, doctors, congressmen like yourself and one day president, so we can make a change to not just the state of South Carolina but also the world." "We are not quitters," she closed.

For the event, Mrs. Obama wore a plum silk and wool dress by Narciso Rodriguez; the dress had first been glimpsed a month before during an inauguration ceremony at Arlington National Cemetery. With a gathered silk top and high-waisted wool skirt, the dress almost resembled separates. The silhouette was hallmark Narciso Rodriguez: clean lines executed in ultra-luxurious fabrics, with a resulting look that was streamlined yet feminine.

In an interview with *Women's Wear Daily*, the designer said of the first lady: "She's such an elegant woman, and that speaks volumes about her. It's something that comes very natural to her, and she makes the choices she likes, and therefore always looks very comfortable and very right."

A public discussion centered on the lack of sleeves in Mrs. Obama's outfit. Robin Givhan, Pulitzer prize-winning fashion writer for the *Washington Post,* described Mrs. Obama as having "post-Title IX arms." Noting the winter temperature in Washington, D.C., that night, Anya Strzemien of the *Huffington Post* thought the sleeveless look displayed Mrs. Obama's "flinty, Chicago toughness." Others noted that in 1963, First Lady Jacqueline Kennedy had worn a sleeveless dress when her husband delivered his State of the Union address. Then and now, the results were the same: both first ladies stood out in a crowd of coats, turtlenecks and buttoned-up suits. They appeared youthful, optimistic, and thoroughly modern.

WEDNESDAY, FEBRUARY 25, 2009

FOR A SPECIAL AWARDS CEREMONY, Michelle Obama welcomed a singer she greatly admired—Stevie Wonder—to the White House. The event honored the music legend, the recipient of the 2nd Annual Gershwin Award for Lifetime Achievement from the Library of Congress. The prize celebrates "the work of an artist whose career reflects lifetime achievement in promoting song as a vehicle of musical expression and cultural understanding."

Library of Congress
Gershwin Award

Mrs. Obama wore an emerald green silk chiffon cocktail dress by L.A.-based designer Kai Milla. The sleeveless bodice featured a deep V-neck with hand-pleated detail, while the skirt had a cascading flow. Originally a full-length gown, the dress was shortened to hit just below the knee for the occasion. Mrs. Obama added a black satin belt to the waist, and accessorized with Loree Rodkin bangles and silver open-toe heels.

The choice of dress was full of meaning. Kai Milla is not only a talented designer, she is also Stevie Wonder's wife. Perfectly chosen for the festive evening, Mrs. Obama's dress also showed thoughtful appreciation for her guests.

"Tonight is a huge thrill for me as we honor a man whose music and lyrics I fell in love with when I was a little girl," Mrs. Obama said prior to introducing the singer. "Years later, when I discovered what Stevie meant about love, Barack and I chose the song 'You and I' as our wedding song."

ABOVE:
Emerald green silk chiffon used in Kai Milla's design.

Kai Milla knows a thing or two about Washington style—she grew up in the nation's capital and attended the Corcoran School, where she studied fine art and design. Her artistic talent led to an early career as an art director and graphic designer in the recording industry, but Kai soon found her true calling in fashion.

In addition to being a prominent designer, Kai is also married to one of music's finest—the legendary Stevie Wonder. First Lady Michelle Obama is a fan of the power couple. She notably wore an emerald green dress by Kai Milla on the February 2009 evening Stevie Wonder was honored at the White House with a Library of Congress award.

Q: What made you want to start your own label?
A: I was already married to Stevie, and I had Kailand, who is seven years old now. I was designing for a lot of private clients, which I was able to do on my own time. But after we had Kailand, I started to get that urge—that I wanted it to be a full-on business. I said, "once Kailand hits two, I'm going."

We started in my house. I took up a whole section of my house, so that I could stay with the baby. As we started to grow, I took over a portion of my husband's studio. At one point he said, "It's time for you to get your own space," so I got my own space.

Around that time, I was in Paris and saw one of Galliano's shows [for Dior]. I was just blown away by the creativity. To see it all come together—it was just, "Wow!" I decided that I wanted to do a show, and we've been growing from there.

Q: How do you want women to feel in your designs?
A: One of the things that's really important to me—as a mother and a woman who travels and is constantly on the go—you want things to be as seamless and effortless as possible. So the clothes have to be easy to get on and easy to travel with, but they still need to look great.

I want women to feel confident in my designs—and a little sexy, here and there. I do like showing parts of the body that I think are really beautiful on women. It could be the back. If I do show the back, then I'm not showing so much on the front. So it's timeless, but at the same time, a little edgy.

Q: What did it mean to you as a designer that the first lady of the United States wore one of your designs?
A: I was over the moon . . . For any designer to have the first lady of the United States wear something of yours, when she has so many options to choose from, it shows she has really opened up her style sensibility to so many designers. And being chosen as one of the designers, I was just taken aback. This is really amazing for me.

Q: Were you in attendance?
A: I was. But I didn't know she was wearing the dress until she walked out. I looked said to my husband, "I think she's wearing my dress." He goes, "Really?" And I said, "Yes!" When we all went to one of the rooms, Michelle Obama and I walked up to each other, nodding our heads in approval. I told her, "You look amazing," and she said, "Thank you, I love it." It was very fresh and chic.

Q: Were there details we might have missed in photographs that were visible in person?
A: The fabric actually has three different silk threads: a green, a reddish-orange, and a black. So it has an amazing, iridescent color that pops. It's a really beautiful color, and it really worked with her. The V-neck was all hand pleated, and it had the same effect in the back. The back actually went to an even deeper V-shape.

Q: There was a wonderful message in the choice of your dress, given your husband was being honored that evening.
A: I think you're absolutely right, and you're on to something. It's a way of showing respect. It signals, "I'm recognizing you, I'm connected with you."

Green Silk Dress
"WaterFall" Back
Black Satin Trim

THURSDAY, MARCH 5, 2009

Miriam's Kitchen

BECOMING INVOLVED WITH HER NEW LOCAL COMMUNITY, Michelle Obama visited Miriam's Kitchen, a non-profit organization that provides meals to the homeless in Washington, D.C. She not only greeted visitors to the kitchen, but she also helped to serve lunch.

"There is a moment in time when each and every one of us needs a helping hand," said Mrs. Obama. She described Miriam's Kitchen as "an example of what we can do as a country and a community to help folks when they're down."

For her visit, she paired a white ruffle blouse, from the new Liz Claiborne New York collection designed by Isaac Mizrahi, with a salmon-pink cardigan sweater by J.Crew. Completing the outfit were black pants and a clear vinyl belt by French designer Sonia Rykiel.

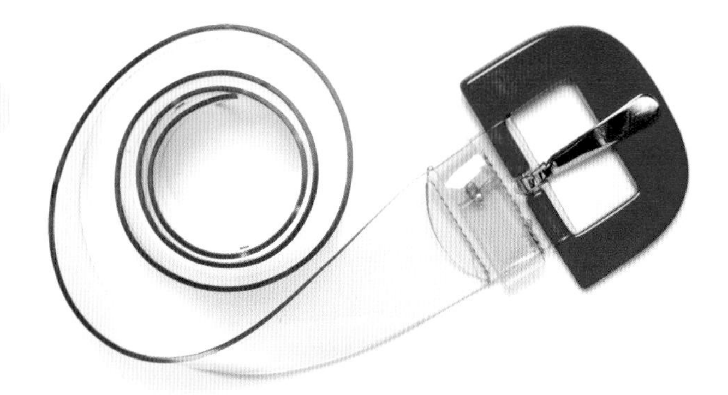

ABOVE:
Clear vinyl belt with distinctive D-shape buckle by Sonia Rykiel.

Isaac Mizrahi championed a movement that changed the American fashion industry forever. Through his influence, a wonderful jacket or great pair of jeans could suddenly be found at Target, at a price almost everyone could afford. In 2008, he signed on as creative director for mid-price American sportswear brand Liz Claiborne. All the while, he continues to produce high-end runway collections for both women and men. He is the king of democratic fashion—and now, he's dressed First Lady Michelle Obama.

Q: What made you want to be a designer?

A: I don't know that I really made a choice. I feel like it's something that I do. It was living in the house, growing up with my mother and two sisters—and how fashion obsessed everyone was in that house. And somehow being the only boy, I became a tyrant. I became the authority in the house about what to wear and how to wear it. That's how I became a fashion designer.

My father was a manufacturer of children's clothes and there were many sewing machines around me growing up. He collected beautiful sewing machines. That sounds fancy. He didn't collect them, they just happened to be around. Before I ever set foot at Parsons, I could run a Merrow machine. People used to come to me with their projects to Merrow, because Merrow can be very devastating. It can have a devastating effect if you do it wrong. Everybody was so scared of the Merrow machine and I was a whiz.

Q: Given that your background and early business was in high fashion, what made you first want to do a collection for the masses?

A: Well, you know, I am from a generation of style people that doesn't just buy expensive clothes at face value. We don't buy the fact that they're better because they're expensive. We test things. We're very skeptical of beauty and truth and the ultimate luxury of something. We don't just take it at face value, just because it's expensive and just because the majority likes it. It has to pass the test of posterity.

Given that, I believe that the simplest thing that costs 50 cents can be just as beautiful and luxurious as something that costs $3,000. Because luxury is not just the face value of something. It's the depth, the inner meaning, the quantity that it weighs on earth. A great T-shirt is a great T-shirt, a great slice of pizza is a great pizza, you know?

That was a big, formative part of my education. Watching ladies like Tina Chow and Maxime de la Falaise and her daughter Loulou, the way they mixed things—the way they had such respect for meager little things and absolutely no respect for grand things. It was just a very good lesson to learn from those ladies.

Q: How did you decide to do the line for Target?

A: It felt right. It felt like a paradigm that was right in the midst of shifting and that I would maybe be on the leading edge of it. I remember being at a restaurant and suddenly this SUV pulled up, a Toyota SUV, and out came the Miller sisters [Pia Getty; Marie Chantal, Crown Princess of Greece; and Alexandra von Furstenberg]. And I thought, "My God, the Miller sisters are not coming out of a big stretch limo, they're coming out of a SUV." I thought, "Well, the world is changing."

Q: And recently you've moved on to Liz Claiborne. What attracted you to the brand?

A: I took the job on the eve of the Obama thing. It was something that I felt was going to change the world. I kind of had this weird psychic prediction that he was going to win. At first I thought it was going to be Hillary, and after she lost the primary, I thought "Okay, Obama is going to win."

It's a new start. There's a newness to the way we feel and the way we look. I felt that the words "Liz Claiborne" were just right for this moment. It's a brand that has always stood for value, and a brand that has always been friendly to working, busy women.

To attend the ribbon cutting ceremony for the Metropolitan Museum of Art American Wing in New York City, Mrs. Obama wore a purple silk wool dress and coat from Isaac Mizrahi's Pre-Fall 2009 collection.

Mrs. Obama has remarkable style. And luckily, she's our heroine at the moment. I think she's going to create a certain kind of fashion consciousness. And the word "consciousness" is very good. It implies that we're going to be thinking about it, but it also implies that we're going to thinking about it in the long term. It's not just going to be something that's amusing for five seconds and then gets cast aside.

I do think she's going to have a lasting impression on the world of fashion, I do. The day that she wore my blouse, I thought I would explode with pride.

Q: Speaking of which, what was it like to see the first lady in one of your designs for Liz Claiborne?
A: It was one of intense pleasure and pride. First, she looks so good in clothes, it's amazing. We're so lucky for that. She's so pretty. I don't want to say that she's pretty, but she is. That's all there is to it. Aside from that, everything speaks to a certain kind of . . . she's an icon. She really is exemplary to so many women.

For one, age doesn't seem to enter into the picture. We don't know how old she is. We know she's 45, but to me, she seems like the perfect ageless woman who's right in her prime. That's someone whom I've always designed for. That's one thing I'm doing with Liz Claiborne, I'm perpetuating this 35-year-old-ness. That's who we all are. Michelle Obama is such a great example of that.

Q: Michelle Obama's favorite Azzedine Alaïa belt made quite an impression on you. Why was that?
A: The thing about it, if you talk to Azzedine Alaïa, he too will say that a $5 Chinese slipper can be way better than a $5,000 couture, bejeweled pump from whomever. The man just makes exquisite clothes. That belt, regardless of how much it costs, is pure value. You know it's made by hand and stitched on these perfect machines. That's why that belt represents something of quality. It's not just gorgeous looking, there's a quality to it, a lasting quality. And then to mix it with a J.Crew sweater, I just go mad.

WEDNESDAY, MARCH 11, 2009

Women of Courage Awards

MICHELLE OBAMA JOINED SECRETARY OF STATE HILLARY CLINTON in congratulating the recipients of the State Department's Women of Courage Awards. The awards honor women who "risk their lives to fight for themselves and for their mothers, daughters, sisters, grandmothers and friends," said the first lady. "And in doing so, they create a better society not just for them, but for their fathers, sons, brothers, grandfathers, and husbands."

These awards followed President Obama's signing of an executive order creating a White House Council on Women and Girls. Mrs. Obama also attended that signing. The Council will provide a coordinated federal response to challenges faced by women of all ages.

For both events, Mrs. Obama appeared in monochromatic purple, wearing a tailored jacket by Zero + Maria Cornejo over a sleek purple sheath dress. In the past, Mrs. Obama has worn several Zero + Maria Cornejo jackets of a similar cut: collarless, nipped at the waist by darts and falling to hip length. This particular jacket had been worn during the Whistle Stop Tour on the first day of inauguration festivities. Accenting the neckline of the dress was a satin bow pin in a slightly darker shade of purple. The bow provided a feminine accent to streamlined, minimalist lines of the dress and the jacket. Black patent leather kitten heels completed her look.

FRIDAY, MARCH 20, 2009

White House Garden

PUTTING ACTION BEHIND HER VERBAL COMMITMENT TO PROMOTE HEALTHY EATING, Mrs. Obama broke ground for a White House vegetable garden. A group of fifth grade students from Bancroft Elementary School in the District of Columbia were invited to help her. The garden would include a medley of vegetables, greens, berries, and herbs that the students would later help to plant, harvest, and cook. Future plans for the garden included an apiary, to be cultivated for honey.

"A real delicious heirloom tomato is one of the sweetest things that you'll ever eat," Mrs. Obama told the *New York Times*. "And my children know the difference, and that's how I've been able to get them to try different things. I wanted to be able to bring what I learned to a broader base of people. And what better way to do it than to plant a vegetable garden in the South Lawn of the White House?"

For her gardening attire, Mrs. Obama wore a long black wrap sweater finished with one of her signature belts, black leggings, and black patent leather boots by Jimmy Choo. The look was both chic and practical. It was also a look that could be easily emulated by fans of the first lady's fashion sense.

From the White House blog: "This is a big day," said Mrs. Obama. "We've been talking about it since the day we moved in." In April, the group would reconvene to plant the garden.

ABOVE:
Michelle Obama and students plant the White House garden in early April.

CHAPTER VII EUROPEAN TOUR

Style Diplomacy

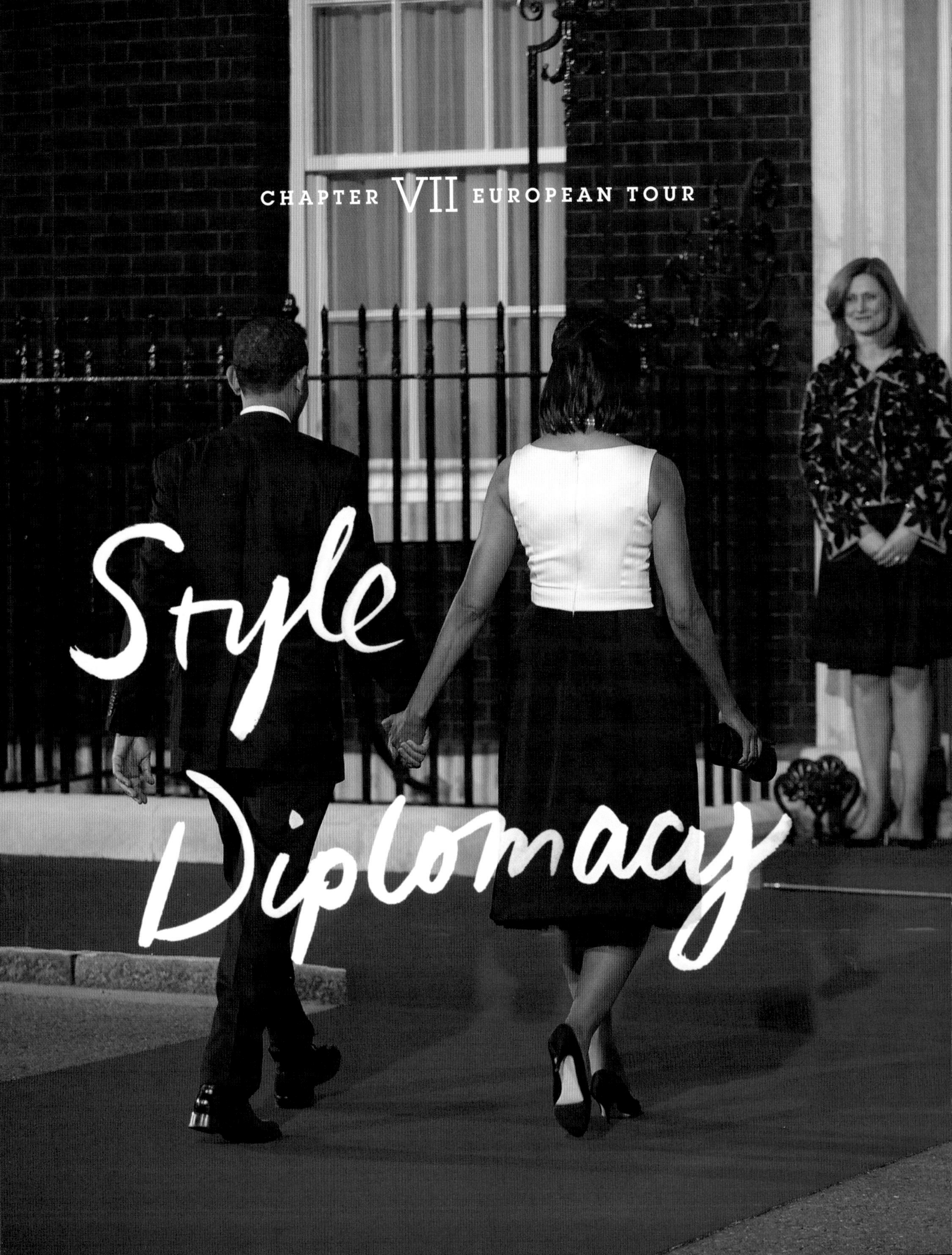

During the early days of April 2009, the Obamas made their first overseas trip to Europe as president and first lady of the United States. While the world economy would be the primary focus of the official trip, there was no shortage of historic first meetings and high-wattage glamour.

The itinerary included stops in London, England; Strasbourg, France; Baden-Baden, Germany; and Prague, Czech Republic. The president would later continue on to Anakara and Istanbul, Turkey, while Mrs. Obama returned to Washington to rejoin her young daughters.

For months, Europe had watched the Obamas from a distance with interest and admiration. Through this trip, Europeans would get to know the president and first lady on a more personal basis, as the couple met with dignitaries, spoke to local groups and explored their host nations' cultural sites and traditions.

The charming and chic Michelle Obama was central to the Obamas' warm reception. At Buckingham Palace, Mrs. Obama met with Queen Elizabeth II, who by the end of their visit, requested that Mrs. Obama "stay in touch." Throughout the week, the first lady enthusiastically engaged with her counterpart spouses, touring London with Sarah Brown, wife of the United Kingdom Prime Minister Gordon Brown; and exploring sites in Strasbourg, France, with French first lady, Carla Bruni-Sarkozy. But it was not just royals and dignitaries who were won over. At a school in North London, a group of young girls clamored with delight as Mrs. Obama knelt down on the stage to give them hugs.

As the trip, in part, served to improve the image of the United States overseas, due credit should be given to the lasting visual impact of Michelle Obama's wardrobe. Mrs. Obama's ensembles for the week were rigorously planned, with an eye for symbolism and gesture. On its own merit, her wardrobe generated media attention around the world, and helped to further propel several of her favorite American designers onto the world stage.

Washington, D.C.

IN THE WEEK LEADING UP TO OBAMAS TRIP OVERSEAS, the first lady had kept a low profile, enjoying an extended stay at Camp David while Malia and Sasha Obama were on spring break. By the time March 31 arrived, anticipation of the trip had reached near fever pitch on both sides of the Atlantic.

While the outcome of the G-20 and NATO summits were top of mind, so too were the scheduled meetings with Queen Elizabeth of the United Kingdom and the Sarkozys of France. By the time Mrs. Obama debuted her first ensemble of the week, her wardrobe was already the subject of international media attention.

As the president and first lady left the White House to board Marine One for Andrews Air Force Base, Mrs. Obama wore a custom-designed, ivory flocked tulle coat with black grosgrain piping by Thakoon Panichgul. The contrasting trim and tweed-like material gave the knee-length coat characteristics reminiscent of a classic '60s-era Chanel jacket. An oversize, jeweled brooch in deep magenta and purple stones popped against the ivory fabric. Beneath the coat, Mrs. Obama wore a Michael Kors double face black wool, cap sleeve sheath dress, accented by Jimmy Choo black kitten heels, diamond stud earrings, and a double-strand pearl necklace. The look had a regal, stately polish.

Six hours later, as Air Force One touched down in London, Mrs. Obama debuted a fresh, new look for that evening. She was dressed in a chartreuse-yellow, silk crepe cocktail dress by Jason Wu, topped by a black, collarless cardigan coat by Michael Kors and her studded Azzedine Alaïa belt at the waist.

The first lady's mid-flight wardrobe change foreshadowed the fashion that would follow. The week would showcase different facets of the first lady's style: from demure to daring, refined to whimsical, vintage-inspired to avant garde—all worn with panache and radiating an inherent glamour.

London, England

FOR HER FIRST DAY IN LONDON, Mrs. Obama joined Sarah Brown, wife of the United Kingdom Prime Minister Gordon Brown, to visit Maggie's Caring Cancer Centre at Charing Cross. Maggie's Centre is a resource devoted to helping cancer patients and their families with the problems associated with the disease. Sarah Brown helped to open the center in April 2008, and is Maggie's official patron.

Maggie's Centre

On the day Mrs. Obama and Mrs. Brown visited, the London center was celebrating its first anniversary, having helped more than 12,000 visitors in its time since opening. During their visit, the two women also spent time at the center's "Look Good, Feel Better" program, which helps cancer patients deal with the appearance-related side effects of cancer, offering skin-care tips and make-up lessons. Mrs. Obama's own make-up artisit, Ingrid Grimes Myles, participates in the same program in Chicago.

Over a cup of tea with the center's staff, the first lady described Maggie's as ". . . an oasis that's necessary for people who are struggling."

For her visit, the first lady dressed in a pastel J.Crew ensemble that projected the promise of spring, and showed sensible deference to the economy. Mrs. Obama wore the brand's Crystal constellation cardigan, embellished with clusters of glass beads, rhinestones, and sequins. The cotton sweater was paired with the brand's Dazzling-dots pencil skirt in mint green jacquard. Mrs. Obama accessorized the look with a double strand of pearls, a stack of beaded and bangle bracelets, and snakeskin Jimmy Choo pumps.

As had been the case when Mrs. Obama appeared on *The Tonight Show* in head to toe J.Crew, the look—and relatively accessible price point of the J.Crew pieces—sent women running to their nearest computer. The J.Crew constellation cardigan sold out on jcrew.com by 10AM the same morning, generating a 200-person wait list by the end of the week.

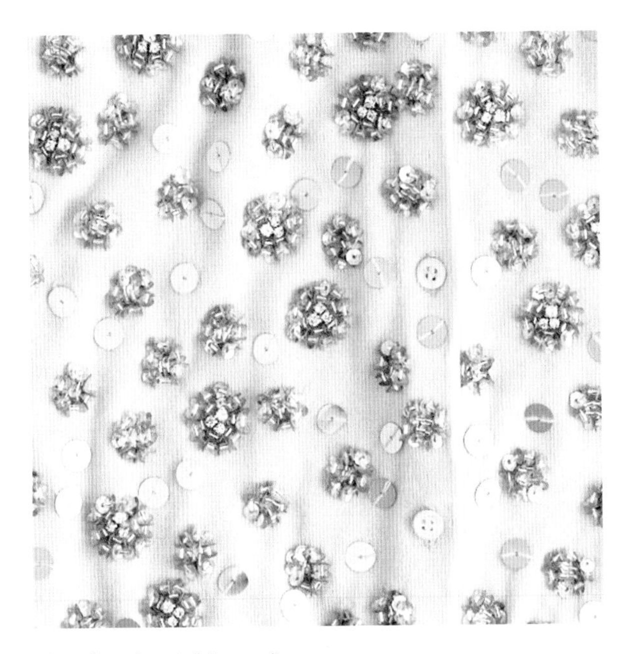

J.Crew Crystal constellation cardigan.

Jimmy Choo Jade pump in snakeskin.

WEDNESDAY, APRIL 1, 2009

Tea with the Queen, G-20 Summit Dinner

AS FIRST LADY MICHELLE OBAMA WALKED INTO BUCKINGHAM PALACE, she was a vision of understated elegance. The first lady wore a black, duchess satin opera coat with a pleated collar by Jason Wu—the sheen of the fabric and volume of the coat pronounced against the gray stone backdrop. With the front of her hair swept up, she carried a small roll clutch and wore dress pumps, both in coordinating black satin.

Inside Buckingham Palace, Mrs. Obama removed her coat, revealing an ivory and black silk crepe dress with an origami-inspired bow detail at the waistline, designed by Isabel Toledo. The fitted bodice and full skirt of the dress, the latter supported by an under layer of tulle petticoat, paired with a cashmere cardigan by Azzedine Alaïa, gave the ensemble a youthful charm.

Of note, both the dress and coat were originally made for different events during the inauguration. The black satin coat by Jason Wu was designed to be worn with Mrs. Obama's Inaugural Ball gown, later replaced by a second and different design in ivory. The dress by Isabel Toledo had been made for the morning church service prior to the oath of office, though Mrs. Obama would ultimately opt to wear the lemongrass ensemble throughout the day. They proved to be a perfect, if unintended, pairing—both with a classic, timeless quality that was ideal for meeting the Queen.

Isabel Toledo was pleased that the ivory and black dress had been saved for the later occasion. "I thought it was perfect," she said. "Michelle Obama really let the Queen shine in her blossom pink." Commenting on the ivory and black palette, Toledo added, "This classic combination is well understood by men in tuxedos. You are always at your best without upstaging anyone else in the room. It is the art of restraint. For a woman, there is a sense of beauty in being discreet."

Later in the evening, Mrs. Obama transitioned her look from day to evening, removing her cardigan for the G-20 Summit dinner at 10 Downing Street, the Prime Minister's residence.

ABOVE: President Barack Obama and First Lady Michelle Obama, in an Isabel Toledo dress and Azzedine Alaïa cardigan, pose for a photo with Queen Elizabeth II at Buckingham Palace.

RIGHT: The Obamas join Prime Minister Gordon Brown and his wife Sarah for the G-20 dinner at 10 Downing Street, the U.K. Prime Minister's official residence.

Elizabeth Garrett Anderson School

FOR HER FINAL DAY IN LONDON, First Lady Michelle Obama would make her boldest fashion statement of the week. Wearing a teal blue, full-skirted dress by Jason Wu, and accessorizing with a double strand of pearls, the foundation of the look had the makings of a traditional ensemble.

Mrs. Obama, however, added an original and fashion forward twist, pairing her dress with an asymmetric, argyle cardigan by avant garde Japanese designer Junya Watanabe. The cardigan hailed from a recent collection themed around Africa, which was expressed using rich colors and prints. The designer, Mr. Watanabe, said of Mrs. Obama's choice: "I was very delighted. I was very pleased to see the free and creative way she chooses her wardrobe." Green Jimmy Choo Glacier pumps, the same worn during the inauguration, completed the ensemble.

While the basic components—a dress paired with a cardigan—had become a trusted silhouette for Mrs. Obama, the choice of cardigan and its designer, demonstrated a unique style sensibility. While much of the week was steeped in custom and tradition with clothes to suit, this particular ensemble showed Mrs. Obama's personality, projecting a certain verve.

The morning would be spent with the G-20 spouses, first touring the Royal Opera House in Covent Garden, where the group listened to a reading by *Harry Potter* author JK Rowling and watched a dance reheasal for the production "Giselle." For the afternoon, the group would visit the Elizabeth Garrett Anderson School in Islington in North London.

There, Mrs. Obama listened to the Girls' Choir perform. Visibily moved, the first lady would tell the girls, "All of you are jewels. You are precious, and you touch my heart."

The first lady continued with words of encouragement, "I was surrounded by extraordinary women in my life who taught me about quiet strength and dignity. . . .You too can control your own destiny, please remember that. Whether you come from a council estate or a country estate, your success will be determined by your own confidence and fortitude."

As Mrs. Obama prepared to leave, girls in the audience rushed to the edge of stage to meet her. Handshakes quickly became hugs, accompanied by shrieks of delight. Mrs. Obama, showing her warm and generous spirit, crouched down to embrace the girls.

Ikram: a fashion force that can be summed up with one word. It is the name of the definitive high-fashion Chicago boutique, and it is the first name of the woman who sartorially knows Michelle Obama best. Since opening her namesake boutique in 2002, Ikram Goldman has been fearlessly pursuing her fashion vision.

Goldman has the courage of her convictions, bringing in a unique mix of American, European, and Japanese designers—including Alexander McQueen, Lanvin, Comme des Garcons, Narciso Rodriguez, Thakoon, Peter Soronen, Azzedine Alaïa and Rodarte. Her jewelry designers include Tom Binns and Loree Rodkin. Yes, the clothes and jewelry can be purchased at other places, too, but here they are brought together under one roof and edited by one discerning eye. The *New York Times* has called Goldman's store, "impossibly chic."

"Ikram has a great eye, one of the best," said Joan Weinstein to *Chicago* magazine. "She has a rare capacity to do both big picture concepts and small details." Weinstein would know. She was the powerhouse behind Ultimo, the fashion-forward Chicago boutique that brought great cutting edge design to the Midwest for 30 years. Goldman, who moved from Israel to Chicago when she was 14, worked at Ultimo—mainly in the women's section but sometimes on the men's floor—under Weinstein's tutelage for a decade. Weinstein retired in 1999, and Ultimo changed hands and, to some degree, direction. A few years later, Goldman opened her own boutique around the corner and began securing exclusive Midwestern rights to well-known designers.

Michelle Obama started shopping at Ikram some time in 2006; she was wearing Sonia Rykiel suits, Noir chiffon blouses, and the now well-known Alaïa black belt by then. (Goldman respectfully declines all questions about her famous customer.) Over time, Mrs. Obama began to turn more and more to fashion choices from Goldman's boutique. At the Democratic National Convention, Mrs. Obama wore designers from Ikram three nights out of four—and even the Pinto dress she wore for her opening night speech had been styled by Goldman. The trend continued during the fall campaign; on election night, Mrs. Obama wore a black and red Narciso Rodriguez dress and an Alaïa cardigan that set the country buzzing. The influence of Goldman on Mrs. Obama's fashion choices became clear during the inauguration festivities, when Mrs. Obama wore a pantheon of designers from Ikram: Isabel Toledo, Jason Wu, Narciso Rodriguez and jewelry from Loree Rodkin and vintage collector Carole Tanenbaum.

Goldman continues to be a hands-on fashion resource to Mrs. Obama as she settles into her role as first lady. Anyone who has ever shopped at the Ikram boutique knows why. Goldman is no fashion dictator, imposing an identifiable template on every customer. Instead, she encourages her customers to play with fashion and to have fun.

Ikram the boutique expands the fashion possibilities for anyone who shops there. That is because Ikram the woman believes that the magic of fashion is all about the mix.

ABOVE:
Michelle Obama wears a Junya Watanabe cardigan for Take Your Child to Work Day.

Asymmetric argyle cardigan in magenta by Junya Watanabe.

ON THEIR TOUR OF EUROPE, the Obamas next traveled to Strasbourg, France. There, President Obama joined a summit of world leaders from NATO countries, where the group would mark the 60th year of the North Atlantic Treaty Organization and plan for the future of the military alliance.

NATO Summit
Strasbourg, France

French President Nicolas Sarkozy and his wife Carla Bruni-Sarkozy welcomed leaders and their spouses to Strasbourg at the Palais Rohan, a cultural hub and prized example of Baroque architecture. The introduction between First Lady Michelle Obama and Carla Bruni-Sarkozy had become one of the most highly anticipated events of the week, as it brought two of the world's most stylish women, face to face, ensemble to ensemble.

For their first meeting, Mrs. Obama wore a custom floral silk jacquard coat by Thakoon with a coordinating, reverse print dress underneath. The hem and sleeves of the dress were trimmed in black mesh elastic. The dress and coat, in fact, were originally designed for consideration on Inauguration Day. While American designers were championed throughout the week, it was a shining moment for Thakoon Panichgul. In a country where fashion is deeply entrenched in the nation's culture and held to fastidious standards, it was high-profile recognition of the young American designer's talent.

Ms. Carla Bruni-Sarkozy wore a gray lambskin coat over a charcoal gray, cap sleeve dress, both by Dior. As it happened, both women's coats featured a soft tie at the neck—a detail that, no doubt coincidental, made them appear stylistically in tune. By all accounts, the first ladies had a pleasant visit. "They had lunch together and a lively conversation," Katie McCormick Lelyveld, Michelle Obama's press secretary said. "They got along very well."

"Mrs. Obama's decision to wear American fashion helps to promote the industry both nationally and internationally.

ANDREW BOLTON, CURATOR,
THE COSTUME INSTITUTE,
THE METROPOLITAN MUSEUM OF ART

NATO Summit Dinner

FOR THE NATO SUMMIT DINNER IN BADEN-BADEN, GERMANY, just over the French-German border, leaders from the 28-member NATO nations gathered for a concert and working dinner.

The dinner was hosted at Kurhaus Casino in Baden-Baden, once described by Marlene Dietrich as "the most beautiful casino in the world." An after-dinner concert followed, with a performance by renowned German violinist Anne-Sophie Mutter, who played a selection of European and American music.

For the event, First Lady Michelle Obama wore a black knit dress with a ruffled skirt and tulle underlay. Mrs. Obama paired the dress with a knit bolero jacket. Both pieces were designed by famed French-Tunisian designer, Azzedine Alaïa. Mrs. Obama accessorized her ensemble with a black heels, diamond hoop earrings and a cuff bracelet.

Born in Tunisia, designer Azzedine Alaïa moved to France to study sculpture at Ecole des Beaux-Arts. Developing his craft as a designer, he would spend two years at Guy Laroche in Paris to learn tailoring. He later went on to establish his own business, known for his attention to the female form and fine craftsmanship. Many would describe him as a master and as "the last true couturier."

"She wore it well," Azzedine Alaïa told *Woman's Wear Daily*. "I couldn't hope for better. She has a very strong presence and has set a new style for first ladies. I'm sure women will follow her style—it's simple and elegant."

Though Mrs. Obama had worn pieces from European designers in the past, the choice of Alaïa represented one of her most high profile departures from American fashion. It seemed a thoughtful sartorial gesture, undoubtedly made to show respect for her host nation France (even if, technically, across the border for the evening) and its legendary designer.

DESPITE HEATED ANTI-WAR AND ANTI-CAPITALIST PROTESTS, First Lady Michelle Obama and the other NATO spouses managed to proceed with their tour of Strasbourg. A trip to a cancer research center was canceled due to the rioting, replaced by an impromptu stop for coffee at the Palais Rohan.

Palais Rohan and Notre Dame Cathedral

Mrs. Obama was the final guest to arrive at the Palais Rohan for the event, hosted by Ms. Carla Bruni-Sarkozy. In greeting one another, the women briefly held hands and gave each other a double-cheek kiss, as is a cultural custom in France.

Following their coffee, the group visited Strasbourg's Notre Dame Cathedral, an 11th century monument and prime example of Gothic architecture. Mrs. Obama and Ms. Bruni-Sarkozy engaged in conversation as they walked side by side through the historic city center.

In regard to wardrobe, Mrs. Obama had again turned to Azzedine Alaïa, this time in the form of a tailored jacket. The double-breasted cropped black jacket displayed signs of fine craftsmanship, particularly in the punched and woven leather seam details. The jacket, in fact, was an existing piece in Mrs. Obama's wardrobe, worn publicly at least once before, during a campaign speech in January 2008.

Beneath the jacket, Mrs. Obama wore a floral cardigan by Etro, white blouse by Moschino, and black trousers by Gunex. Her silver-studded belt was by Sacai, a Japanese design house based in the Marais district of Paris. In a single ensemble, the first lady had managed to support five European-based designers. Brunello Cucinelli, founder of his namesake Italian company that produces Gunex, told *Woman's Wear Daily*, "I love Michelle Obama because she is beautiful, energetic, and has a strong presence."

As the stop in Strasbourg came to a close, it was by all accounts a success. As a gesture of appreciation to her host, Mrs. Obama presented Ms. Carla Bruni-Sarkozy with a Gibson guitar, a thoughtful acknowledgment of her musical talents.

SUNDAY, APRIL 5, 2009

Prague,
Czech Republic

ON THE MORNING OF THE OBAMAS' FINAL DAY TOGETHER IN EUROPE, President Obama would give a public speech at the main entrance of Prague Castle. More than 20,000 locals crowded into the surrounding area, greeting the Obamas with a warm welcome of cheers and applause. Two such supporters were Dave Watson and Kathleen Noonan, an American couple who has lived in Prague for the past four years. The pair was fortunate enough to have a brief conversation with First Lady Michelle Obama as she circled through the crowd.

The first lady was dressed in a white blouse with an oversize bow by Moschino, paired with a black cardigan, Michael Kors black pencil skirt, and her signature Azzedine Alaïa studded belt. The bow blouse, the focal point of the ensemble, originated from Moschino's Spring 2009 collection.

In conversation with Mrs. Obama, Ms. Noonan commented, "Love the bow." The first lady acknowledged, "It's a big bow," continuing with a smile, "If you're going to do a bow, I think it should be a *big* bow." While Mrs. Obama had shown different sides to her style throughout the week, her final sartorial gesture would project a fun and playful spirit.

Hosted by Czech First Lady Livia Klausová, Mrs. Obama spent the rest of her day exploring the cobblestone streets of Prague, taking in a range of the city's cultural landmarks.

They spent several hours touring the city's Jewish Quarter, including the Pinkas Synagogue. At the Old Jewish Cemetery, the site of 12,000 family gravestones near the Vltava River, Mrs. Obama honored local tradition by inscribing a prayer on paper and securing it with a small stone.

Mrs. Obama's last stop was the Old New Synagogue. Completed in the 13th century, it is the oldest active synagogue in Europe and one of the first Gothic buildings in Prague. While Mrs. Obama had clearly made an impression on Prague, the feeling was quite mutual. "It was a wonderful visit, but much too short," the first lady told the city's Jewish leaders. "I'll be back."

Oversize bow blouse from Moschino's Spring 2009 collection.

CHAPTER VIII

Expert Reflections

Obamas walking Bo
on White House lawn.

Wendy Donahue **is a fashion writer for the *Chicago Tribune*. She has seen the influence of Michelle Obama's style up and down the Magnificent Mile, and offers firsthand perspective on the booming Chicago fashion scene.**

Q: What influence have you seen Michelle Obama's style have on Chicago women?

A: I see women taking chances they didn't a year ago. Wearing a green shoe as a neutral, for example. Chicago style is more conservative than, say, New York, in terms of spending, but also in terms of how clothes are worn. I can admit readily that I've been influenced by Michelle's example. I'm taking more risks than a year ago—not being so matchy-matchy. It's making fashion really fun again.

Q: How would you describe Michelle Obama's style?

A: Friendly, approachable, independent—almost to rebellion. Imperfect in a charming way. She operates on tastes and instincts, and doesn't follow the crowd. She's become known for blending high and low. She doesn't show any more or less reverence to J.Crew than Jason Wu.

Some critics are frustrated by her fallibility. For people who admire her, though, her example has been really liberating. Women are realizing that Michelle can stumble with her fashion choice one evening and get up the next morning and triumph, and still be the same person she was in either instance.

Q: How would you describe Chicago style?

A: There's an independence from the dictates of fashion. Women buy fashion as an investment. They don't buy a bag to throw aside after one season. It's not about wearing the brand or designer of the moment. Investments are made in more classic shapes and silhouettes. You wear something because you truly like it and it suits you.

Q: What role do boutiques like Ikram and designers like Maria Pinto have on the Chicago style scene?

A: Ikram appreciates artistry and the avant garde. Her design aesthetic makes us think. She has done wonders for raising Chicago's fashion profile. She has shown the world—which was not her mission necessarily—that there is a market and customer in Chicago for the most innovative designers. Even before Michelle Obama, Ikram was getting credits in *Vogue* and *Harper's Bazaar*.

FAR LEFT: For the White House Correspondents Dinner, Michelle Obama wears a Michael Kors magenta dress in double face stretch wool crepe, paired with a St. Erasmus necklace made of fresh water pearls, Swarovski crystal and Zari thread.

There's a well-known stylist based in Chicago who thinks Ikram's store is one of only a handful in the world that traffic in fashion that is truly advancing the industry. She's been a pioneer in that way.

Even before Ikram there was Joan Weinstein and Ultimo. There have always been sources and a market in Chicago for the most sophisticated fashion, but Chicagoans tend to be discreet about it. Whether they like it or not, Ikram and Michelle Obama are elevating Chicago's profile in the fashion world.

Maria Pinto has a name here and a strong following. She's very familiar, very firmly rooted in the world that real women live in. She is accessible and relatable. Her aim is to make women feel great in their clothes. It's not about making a fashion statement per se, but making a woman really shine in clothes that flatter her body.

Booth Moore is the chief fashion critic for the *Los Angeles Times*. She offers unerring analysis and thought-provoking insight on Michelle Obama's style and its wide-ranging influence.

Q: You were one who gave the Narciso Rodriguez dress on election night a positive review. What was your initial reaction?

A: I thought it was a very fashion-y choice. There wasn't anything safe about it. I did just love the symbolism of the red sort of bursting out of the black. I thought it was dramatic and kind of exciting. It was definitely a declaration that she was going to be a first lady unlike any we've seen recently—right off the bat. She knew already that people were following her style and enjoying what she was wearing. I think she said, "Hey, I like fashion, I like to play with it, and this is who I am, and I'm not going to stop being who I am just because I have this new role."

Q: Later you wrote that the camel and black Narciso Rodriguez ensemble worn for the "We Are One" concert during the inauguration was "strong, elegant and, above all, modern." What gave it that effect?

A: To me it was just a totally new-looking suit. We were used to seeing Mrs. Bush in a traditional three-button blazer and pants, the same with Mrs. Clinton. Here was a dress and coat combo, which is something that can look very sophisticated, but is not your typical women's suit. I also liked the color combination, the black and the camel. I thought it was very graphic against the monument. It was very clean, graphic, sophisticated—a new take on the suit.

Q: What was your reaction to the daytime Isabel Toledo ensemble worn on Inauguration Day?

A: Again, she was sort of taking a risk. Isabel Toledo is a designer that a lot of people don't know. It was a color, one that a lot of people wouldn't wear. It made a statement that she was going to be her own woman and going to have fun with fashion. I thought it was elegant, befitting the occasion. And the color ended up looking fabulous on her.

Q: Any thoughts on the Jason Wu gown worn for the Inaugural Ball?

A: When I first looked at it, I thought "Wow, it's kind of frothy, it looks a bit like a wedding gown." But it did sort of hammer home the message that this was a return to Camelot or to a fairy tale like time in American history. It was very celebratory. And exemplary of the kind of workmanship that can be done here, that people may just think can be done in Europe.

Q: When has Michelle Obama gotten it most right from a style perspective? Do you have a favorite look?

A: I really like the Maria Pinto sheaths that she wears. It's just an example of someone finding a silhouette, a piece that really works for them, and continuing to wear it, and then just throwing on really interesting accessories to make it look different. It's great when people find a signature look and I think the sleeveless sheath dress is really her signature look. That's a good style lesson for people—to find that one thing that works for you, and reinvent it day after day.

Q: How do you think Michelle Obama's style might impact our social history, in the way that American women dress and look at fashion?

A: I think that, in the similar way that Carla Bruni-Sarkozy is giving France a stylish image again, the way that she's doing things—whether its entertaining or the way she's dressing—is boosting America's style quotient. When you look through history and look back at Jackie Kennedy or Frances Cleveland, those were moments when we could feel like we were chic Americans. And she's really making us feel like chic Americans again.

And hopefully, she's sort of giving the American fashion industry the kick in the pants that it needs to have a kind of changing of the guard. You could already see it this past fashion week in New York—the excitement surrounding the runway shows of all the designers that she's worn. You could feel that something had changed . . . that people's interests and priorities had changed . . . that there was this new generation coming up.

RIGHT: For a stroll on the White House lawn, the first lady wears a white, lace-up Azzedine Alaïa blouse and slim black pants.

Robin Givhan **is a Pulitzer Prize-winning fashion editor for the *Washington Post*. In 2009, she plans to relocate from New York to Washington, where she'll observe Michelle Obama's influence firsthand. Her writing extends far beyond fashion commentary, searching for and teasing out the hidden messages and greater social meaning.**

Q: What message do you see the first lady's clothes communicating?

A: Well, I think a lot of it has to do with negotiating the many mine fields related to fashion in this country. We have a very particular and very tortured relationship to fashion as a culture. On the one hand we want to be represented well. I think, as a country, we can be a bit insecure as to how we're perceived on the world stage, whether or not we measure up to older cultures. But at the same time, there is push back with fashion because we perceive it as something that's elitist, or something that's frivolous. There is a puritanical sensibility that we have about fashion.

Somewhere there has to be a happy medium. I think what Michelle Obama has managed to do is to give people the glamour, the sense of modernness and contemporary style, the youth and exuberance—but at the same time grounding it in clothes that say, "I'm not presumptuous. I'm not trying to be the Queen of America," by wearing clothes from H&M and J.Crew. So I think that's part of the message that's being sent.

Q: There's been some criticism that there's too much attention on Michelle Obama's style, and that we're subsequently selling the first lady short in other respects. What do you make of this?

A: Well, I would say that there has been an incredible hunger, and fashion vacuum in Washington for a while. So I think it's understandable that people kind of go overboard when there is the slightest hint of a first lady who is interested in fashion, and seems to enjoy it.

I do think there's a danger in letting it overwhelm everything else. But I don't think that that's happening, and I don't necessarily think that it is something that would happen with Michelle Obama. I tend to believe that if your clothes can become the most scintillating thing that people can find about you, then you're not that scintillating to begin with—and I don't think that's an issue with Michelle Obama.

Q: Why do you think women are so taken with Michelle Obama's style?

A: I don't think that any other first lady in recent memory has injected that much personality, and personal preference into her clothing. She gives the impression that she's dressing in a way that pleases her, as opposed to a way that is meant to be in service to the position. I think for a lot of women, that's what they aspire to, and often, that's where they stumble. To some degree, I think the fascination is: here's a woman who's not losing herself in this conceivably, enormously overwhelming spot that she's in.

We have archetypes in our head about what a successful female politician looks like, or what a successful female lawyer looks like, or what the stay-at-home soccer mom is supposed to look like, and whenever someone doesn't fall into that mold, it obviously makes them stand out and we're intrigued by that.

On Easter Sunday, Michelle Obama wears a custom two-shoulder version of Peter Soronen's lace dress.

One-shoulder painted lace dress from Peter Soronen's Spring 2009 collection.

André Leon Talley **is the American editor-at-large for *Vogue*, and has been a driving force in American fashion for more than 25 years. For the March 2009 issue, he interviewed and profiled First Lady Michelle Obama for a feature piece, "Leading Lady."**

Q: When did you first meet Michelle Obama?
A: At Oprah Winfrey's Legends ball in 2005, which was at her home in California. I first met Mrs. Obama at the dinner on Friday night, the evening before the grand ball.

Q: What were your first impressions?
A: I thought she was a stunning lady, with great confidence. She was articulate, and her conversation was great—not that our conversation was about fashion. It was not. At the time, I only knew that she was a senator's wife from Chicago, but I remember that it was a big deal to have met her. I remember thinking, "This is an extraordinary human being." But we did not keep in touch immediately after that.

Q: So when did your paths cross again?
A: On June 17, 2008, when myself, [*Vogue* editor-in-chief] Anna Wintour, [her partner] Shelby Bryan, and Calvin Klein hosted a fund-raiser for the Obamas in New York City. We raised more than a million dollars for the campaign that evening, and it was splendid.

Q: Was it the same woman you had met at Oprah's house years before? Had she changed?
A: No, not at all. She was still total elegance, just as I had met her. She is a woman who knows exactly who she is, who just exudes warmth and friendship. She looked immaculate as well: in an Isabel Toledo ensemble, with a Tom Binns necklace.

Q: You've said in the past that you didn't think you would see an African American president in your lifetime. At this fund-raiser, were you then thinking it was possible?
A: I was hoping and praying. I worked hard for that dream to become a reality, as did millions and millions of other Americans. To be honest, I had doubts that we could do it—but I did not give up hope.

Q: What are your hopes for Michelle in the fashion arena?
A: She's already achieved it all. On her own shoulders and back and arms, she has redefined what it means to be a first lady. She's made fashion accessible on all levels—from the high, like the Isabel Toledo lemongrass [she wore to the Inauguration], to lower price points, like her J.Crew ensembles. She has a variety, she is flexible, she is American. What could be more American than an American sweater?

Through fashion she has created her own sense of pragmatism and something that people can identify with. People can relate to her not only as a fashion icon, but as a woman and a mother and a wife.

Q: What do you consider to be one of Mrs. Obama's most chicly dressed moments as first lady?
Michelle Obama's choice of a sophisticated, black Alaïa dress and a sweater to wear to New York on a Saturday evening on the town with the president was one of the most elegant and iconic moments in her first year as first lady. She has changed and shifted the paradigm of what elegance and beauty are. Her deportment, her way of turning casual into high style is the most powerful tool in her philosophy of "wear what you love".

Q: Has she ever inquired for your help on matters involving fashion?
A: We have never discussed fashion. We've never had the slightest dialogue about what to wear.

Q: What do you talk about then?
A: Her children. Her role as the first mother of the country. Being an African American woman. Being a woman with influence, a woman of substance. I like what she stands for: you can be a woman, a good wife, and a modern mother. She fills so many shoes. She has her own identity, and she has brought so many things to view in so many different ways.

Take the organic garden she planted at the White House. Mrs. Obama has used this garden as an educational tool, to talk about pesticides and how to prepare one's own vegetables and inspire people to garden in their own homes.

Q: Do you think all this attention paid to her wardrobe will overshadow this agenda?
A: I've heard someone else say that, and I think that's ridiculous. I am not worried about Michelle Obama in the slightest. She is the most capable woman in the world.

For a Cinco de Mayo celebration, Michelle Obama wears a cashmere argyle cardigan by J.Crew, paired with a gray pleated skirt.

CHAPTER IX

The People's Perspective

IN THE RELATIVELY SHORT PERIOD that Mrs. O has been in the public eye, she has inspired millions of people from all over the world. Through Mrs-O.org, we have witnessed a growing affection for the new first lady's style and substance. An overwhelming sense of joy permeates the discussion, whether it's her fresh take on first lady fashion, her strong personality represented in her bold use of color, or her penchant for personalization.

To close this book, the final thoughts come from the fans themselves. Accompanying these thoughts is a selection of artwork inspired by the first lady.

Michelle Obama has brought fashion back to the people. Her bright outfits can inspire people in their 20s or people in their 50s.

Ave. Cambridge, UK

I am profoundly impressed with her choices of American, young and not as well-known designers. I love (and I'm not just throwing that word around) that she shops at the same stores as me. I'm not able to explain why, but it actually fills me with joy and pride that she'll wear J.Crew in front of the world.

Nicole Robinson. London, UK

America for long has been viewed as the country of conspicuous consumption; we acquire materials things as "window dressing," but there's rarely anything inside. Mrs. O shows that while we may look good (and are often in pain for it!), there is substance: a good education, family values, community involvement, strong opinions, and points of view. We haven't had a first lady of Mrs. O's age in some time, and I believe her impact on the meaning of "woman," "America," and "American woman" will be changed forever, and for the better, during President Obama's time in office.

MINDY ROMERO. NEW YORK, NY

Mrs. O somehow tapped into every woman's need for expression through fashion, and coupled it with substance (her promotion of organic gardens in everyone's backyard; of girls' education and hard work; of volunteering for local community services). So she is very savvy in mixing the two (style and substance) because she knows she's in an important position of influence and history in America. She is a much needed role model that is inspirational to all Americans.

VICKY MARKHAM, WILTON, CT

Her choices are democratic and at least semi-accessible — aspirational without being overly intimidating. As a 39-year-old working mom, I know how easy it is to just throw up your hands and grab the first thing off the rack that fits or to get stuck in a style time warp. Maybe I'm overstating it, but I think Michelle's style has inspired a lot of busy women of a certain age to update their wardrobes and have some fun with fashion again.

ERIKA D. PETERMAN. TALLAHASSEE, FL

Despite being 16, I really admire how she doesn't conform to the normal, ill-fitting suit look. She has her own style and mixes affordable things with one-off designer outfits. I hope to dress like her when I am older.

— Cleo, London, England

She has put a stake through the heart of the blood-sucking pantsuit! She's made fresh, contemporary, but appropriate outfits acceptable for professional women who don't want to look like their mothers.

TANNER STRICKLAND LENART. SALT LAKE CITY, UT

MICHELLE

woman, wife, lawyer, mother, first lady

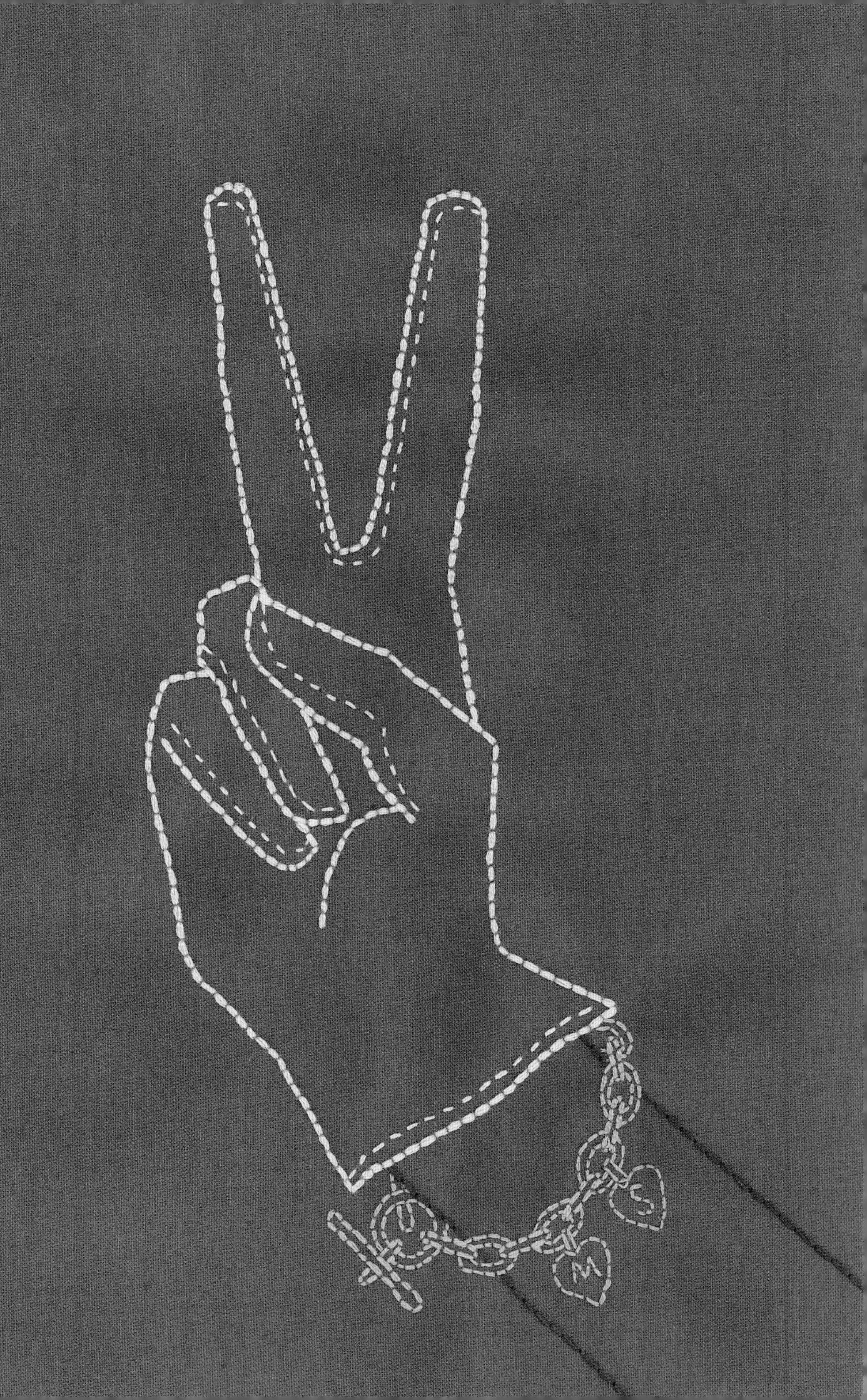

Mrs. O's style is fiercely her own. Her presence of mind is so confident, strong, and secure that she radiates from the inside out. The clothes do not make the woman in this case, and that's what makes Michelle Obama so special.

MELINDA JAMES-LEWIS. HARLEM, NY

I like that she's thinking laterally and trying new designers, thus providing them with a platform they would never ordinarily have. She tries new things and is not afraid to make mistakes.

MELANIE KING. SYDNEY, AUSTRALIA

The reason why Mrs. O's style appeals to so many people is that she is not dressing "above" us. Even when she wore her gown on inauguration night (which was lovely, feminine, and translucently gorgeous) she is one of us. She is streamlined. She is not buttoned up to the neck. She's not trying to pretend to be the first lady. She just is. That's what we all want. Just to be us.

JULIA TANEN. FRANKLIN, MA

I may be a bit unusual among those who obsessively follow Mrs. O, because I am an old, white, quietly feminist woman born in and returned to a conservative area that doesn't fit me, but is inexpensive for retirees. I feel fiercely protective of Barack and Michelle Obama, so I have been shocked on occasion by Mrs. Obama's clothing choices. As a little country girl who worked my way from tiny town to the big state university to the big city of Chicago, I was overly conservative in my clothing choices, so as to display my good taste and conformity as defenses against the scary world. When Mrs. O wore too many patterns, too tight cardigans, colors that don't perfectly match, I was alarmed (the protectiveness). Then, I finally wrote to my 90+-year-old girl cousin, also an Obama voter, that I don't care if Michelle wears a potato sack with jeweled shoes (and a studded belt, of course), I'm just going to enjoy seeing what she does next. If only I had had her dazzling confidence and self-possession and focus on others when I was young—the things that are profoundly more important than the silly details that were alarming me.

GLORIA SCOTT, SPRINGFIELD, MO

I love Mrs. O's style because I can relate to it. As a low-income student and die-hard fashion lover, I am inspired by Mrs. O's elegance and risks to try new and innovative things with my wardrobe. Furthermore, for years I've read books on style great first lady Jackie O and have always wondered what the era of Camelot and style-icon first ladies must have been like. This year, I voted for President Obama's policies and platforms, but I also was thrilled at the prospect of a first lady who had panache and fabulous platforms.

DANIEL PINO. FAIRFAX, VA

Because I love her.

STACEY BURCH. WASHINGTON, DC

ACKNOWLEDGEMENTS

There is a long list of people whose participation and support made this book possible. I would like to thank the following:

Harry Helm and Michelle Rapkin at Center Street, the most wonderful and trusting editors, for their patience, enthusiasm, and extended deadlines.

Eileen Cope at Trident Media Group, New York literary agent extraordinaire, for seeing the potential in this book and helping it to come to fruition.

Rodrigo Corral and Ben Wiseman at Rodrigo Corral Design, two men of remarkable talent who made this book a beautiful, visual feast!

Marcia Froelke Coburn, a talented Chicago-based journalist and writer for Mrs-O.org. Her written contribution to this book, and Chicago perspective, have been invaluable.

Derek Blasberg, senior writer and globetrotter, who secured, conducted, and edited wonderful interviews with Andrew Bolton, André Leon Talley, Thakoon Panichgul and Michael Kors.

BBH, my brave and beloved employer, an advertising agency comprised of the smartest, most creative people I know. They have supported both this book and Mrs-O.org from the very beginning.

At BBH and Zag:
Kevin Roddy, Emma Cookson, Steve Harty, Greg Anderson, Dan Tucker, Joe da Silva, Neil Munn, Ben Malbon, Richard Schatzberger, Jeff Johnson, and Katie Harrison

Most especially:
Ben Jenkins, for his ongoing mentorship and partnership.

Travis Quinn, resident bibliophile, for his discerning, artistic eye.

Sarah Dien, for her patience and pleasant disposition.

Evan Wolfe, who was instrumental in the the 11th hour.

Molly Dowd, for her excellence in photo research, and Virginia Ritchie, a superb, all-around lovely intern—both of whom provided sartorial inspiration on a daily basis.

Tremendous thanks to all of the designers, collectors, and fashion journalists who so graciously gave their time and insightful words. Their collaboration was made possible by all of the talented PR people and business partners who support them.

Andrew Bolton; Jayne Chase; Maria Cornejo, Gabrielle Sirkin, Marysia Woroniecka; Wendy Donahue; Pieter Erasmus; Karen Erickson, Caroline Payne, Chris Shields, Mandie Erickson, Monique Erickson; Robin Givhan; Claire Howorth; Rossella Jardini, Claudia Magic, Michelle Stein, Elisa Brontini, Sarah Monti; Michael Kors, Billy Daley, Molly Biscone; Timothy Long; Jenna Lyons, Lance Lin and Heather McAuliffe; Tamara Mellon, Hannah Lawrence, Lana Silva, Caroline Berthet; Booth Moore; Kai Milla, Kate Goldberg, Tina Malhotra, Lisa Petersen; Isaac Mizrahi, Jennifer Lurie, Sarah Carnabuci, Rachel Freedman; Karen O'Brien, Ashley Futterknecht; Thakoon Panichgul, Lisa Lupinski; Maria Pinto, Mark Davidovich, Laura Verdugo; Pierre Rainero, Erin Collins; Donna Ricco, Kristi Baudone; Patrick Robinson, Sarah Anderson; Loree Rodkin, Marla Bell; Narciso Rodriguez, Jenny Kim, Kate Etter; Carolyn Rosenberg; Sonia Rykiel, Michelle Melton; Peter Soronen, Ellen Carey; André Leon Talley; Carole Tanenbaum; Isabel Toledo, Ruben Toledo; Diane von Furstenberg, Emese Szenasy; Lena Wald, Karen Davis-Weyman; Junya Watanabe, Alexis Liu; Jason Wu, Gina Pepe, Gustavo Rangel; Joe Zee, Akiko Matsuura, Christopher Cunningham, Jed Root

Additionally:

Christina Latargia, Etro; Iliana McGrath, Creativity, Inc.; Jennifer Uglialoro, H&M; Kona Bay Fabrics

The beautiful images in this book would not have been possible without the help of the following:

Ted Ciuzio, AP Images; Nancy Glowinski, Reuters; Craig Granger, Getty Images; Lauren Moosbrugger & Scott Candiotti, Corbis Images; Coral Petretti, Disney/ABC Television Group; Ronald Pledge, Contact Press image; Josette Lata, Josette Lata Represents; Sherry Riad, Radical Media; Bill Stockland, Stockland Martel; Amy Barton, Whitney M. Young Magnet High School

Special thanks to those who submitted illustrations for consideration.

Additional thanks to:

Emma Axling, Ammo Agency; Shereka Evans, Traffic; Karine Garnier and Katja Martinez, Katja Martinez Agency; Petra Koivisto, Pekka; Stephanie Pesakoff, Art Department Illustration Division

Additional thanks to Steven Brinlee, fashion writer, for his copywriting input.

On a personal note, I owe heartfelt thanks to the many wonderful people in my life, who have always been supportive, but remarkably so over the past several months. Most especially: Martha Wiles, my lovely mother, favorite person on earth, and the best writer I know. Mr. Doug-o-las Wiles, for embracing a fashion blog! Jimmy Byun, my dear and great love. And to my wonderful, cherished friends—Alli K., Christa B., Erin G., Erin R. Jen S., Julie B., Kate L., Kim B., Lili D., Lindsay G., Marta L., Maura N., and Meg H.

The community on Mrs-O.org is an absolute inspiration in itself. It was important to capture the articulate, insightful, and varied perspectives of those that visit the site. They make Mrs-O.org the thriving, buzzing online community it has become.

Finally, I owe great thanks to Michelle Obama, first lady of the United States—the woman who unites and inspires us all.

PHOTO CREDITS

Adjacent imagery separated by;
Vertical imagery separated by –

ii: White House Photo/Flickr/Public Domain. vi: White House Photo/Flickr/Public Domain. ix: Mike Baird via Flickr. 1: Whitney M. Young Magnet High School, Chicago. 3: Whitney M. Young Magnet High School, Chicago. 4: (From Top) Nassau Herald, 1985 – Joe Wrinn/Harvard University/Handout/Corbis. 7: Handout from Obama for America via AP. 8: (From Top) Getty Images/Scott J. Ferrell – Getty Images/Scott Olson. 9: Photo by Katrina Wittkamp. 10: (From Top) AP Photo – Getty Images/Simon Maina. 11: Portrait by Timothy Greenfield Sanders/Stockland Martel. 12-13: Getty Images/Charles Ommanney. 15: Jason Reed/Reuters. 16-17: Getty Images/Charles Ommanney. 18-19: Getty Images/Charles Ommanney. 20: Chris Pizzello/Reuters. 21: Getty Images/Cindy Gold. 22-23: Getty Images/Chris Hondros. 25: Getty Images/Chip Somodevilla. 27: Photos by Frank Mullin. 28: AP Photo – Maria Pinto Rachel ruffle blouse, photo by Rodrigo Corral Design/Tracy Morford. 29: AP Photo. 30: John Gress/Reuters. 31: Moschino olive green jacket and skirt, image courtesy of Moschino. 32-33: Getty Images/Charles Ommanney. 34: Getty Images/Emmanuel Dunand. 35: Getty Images/Emmanuel Dunand. 36: Illustration by Rodrigo Corral Design/Ben Wiseman. 37: Photos by Erika Dufour. 39: Getty Images/Marcel Thomas. 40: American Broadcasting Companies Inc. 41: American Broadcasting Companies Inc. 42: Illustration by Rodrigo Corral Design/Ben Wiseman. 43: Donna Ricco black and white print dress, photo by Rodrigo Corral Design/Tracy Morford. 44: Carolyn Rosenberg feather brooch, photo by Rodrigo Corral Design/Michael Schmelling. 45: Getty Images/Chip Somodevilla. 46-47: AP Photo. 48: AP Photo. 49: Moschino floral shirtdress, image courtesy of Moschino. 50-51: Getty Images/Spencer Platt. 53: Getty Images/Robyn Beck. 54: Erickson Beamon, Ltd. Victory Garden brooch in turquoise, photo by Rodrigo Corral Design/Tracy Morford. 55: Maria Pinto, teal V-neck sheath dress, photo by Rodrigo Corral Design/Tracy Morford. 57: AP Photo. 58-59: Erickson Beamon, Ltd. Peace at Last glass pearl necklace, photo by Rodrigo Corral Design/Tracy Morford. 60: (From top) Ivory and lime brocade fabric used by Peter Soronen, photo by Rodrigo Corral Design/Michael Schmelling – Peter Soronen dress, photo provided by Peter Soronen. 61: Getty Images/Justin Sullivan. 62-63: Eric Thayer/Reuters. 64-65: AP Photo. 66-67: (From top) Vernon Bryant/Dallas Morning News/Corbis – Moschino floral sequin brooches, photo by Rodrigo Corral Design/Tracy Morford. 68-69: AP Photo. 71: Getty Images/Joe Raedle. 72-73: AP Photo. 74-75: Thakoon reverse kimono dress, photos by Rodrigo Corral Design/Tracy Morford. 76: Illustration by Rodrigo Corral Design/Ben Wiseman. 77: Erickson Beamon, Ltd. Victory Garden brooches, photo by Rodrigo Corral Design/Tracy Morford. 78: Illustration by Rodrigo Corral Design/Ben Wiseman. 79: Medley or roses by Miho Kosuda, Ltd., photo by Rodrigo Corral Design/Tracy Morford. 80-81: AP Photo. 82-83: AP Photo. 84: Illustration by Rodrigo Corral Design/Ben Wiseman. 85: Zero + Maria Cornejo jacket in evening raffia, photo by Rodrigo Corral Design/Michael Schmelling. 87: Getty Images/Win McNamee. 88: AP Photo. 89: H&M dress, photo by Rodrigo Corral Design/Tracy Morford. 91: Getty Images/Pool. 92: Getty Images/Pool. 93: Getty Images/Emmanuel Dunand. 94-95: Jimmy Choo Glacier pumps, photo by Rodrigo Corral Design/Michael Schmelling. 96: Brett Marty; AP Photo. 97: Hattie Carnegie silk flower pin from the Carole Tanenbaum Vintage Collection, photo by Rodrigo Corral Design/Tracy Morford. 98: AP Photo. 99: AP Photo. 100: Illustration by Rodrigo Corral Design/Ben Wiseman. 101: J. Crew Italian deco tank shirt, photo provided by J. Crew. 102: (From top) Lena Wald peace sign necklace, photo by Rodrigo Corral Design/Tracy Morford – Blue Moon Beads "Hope" charm, photo by Rodrigo Corral Design/Tracy Morford. 103: AP Photo. 105: AP Photo. 106: (Left to Right) Jimmy Choo Jade pump, photo by Rodrigo Corral Design/

Michael Schmelling; Loree Rodkin Triple Constellation earrings, photo supplied by Loree Rodkin. 107: AP Photo. 108-109: AP Photo. 110: John Gress/Reuters. 111: Sonia Rykiel black wool swing coat, photo by Rodrigo Corral Design/Michael Schmelling. 112: Ho New/Reuters. 113: Maria Pinto wool crepe dress, photo by Rodrigo Corral Design/Tracy Morford. 115: American Broadcasting Companies Inc. 116-117: AP Photo. 118: David Burnett/Contact Press Images. 119: Jim Young/Reuters. 120-121: Getty Images/Mandel Ngan. 123: Getty Images/Mark Rolston. 124: Getty Images/Brendan Smialowski. 125: Mike Segar/Reuters/Corbis. 126: Getty Images/Timothy A. Clary. 127: AP Photo. 128: Getty Images/Pool. 129: Getty Images/Robyn Beck. 130-131: Getty Images/Charles Ommanney. 133: Troy House. 134-135: Designs by Isabel Toledo; Illustration by Ruben Toledo. 136: White House Photo/Flickr/Public Domain. 137: Getty Images/Mark Wilson. 138: Illustration by Rodrigo Corral Design/Ben Wiseman. 139: Photo by David B. King. 140-141: White House Photo/Pete Souza. 143: Photo by Christopher Sturman. 144: Kona Bay Fabrics, photo by Rodrigo Corral Design/Michael Schmelling. 145: Getty Images/Jim Watson. 146-147: White House Photo/Flickr/Public Domain. 148: Cartier Tank Francaise steel watch, photo by Rodrigo Corral Design/Michael Schmelling. 149: Getty Images/The White House. 150: Illustration by Rodrigo Corral Design/Ben Wiseman. 151: Getty Images/Kevin Mazur. 153: Kevin Lamarque/Reuters/Corbis. 155: Getty Images/Yuri Gripas. 157: AP Photo. 158: (From Left) Moschino metallic bead brooch, photo by Rodrigo Corral Design/Tracy Morford; Peter Soronen houndstooth jacket, photo by Rodrigo Corral Design/Tracy Morford. 159: Getty Images/Brendan Smialowski. 161: Kevin Lamarque/Reuters/Corbis. 162: Jason Wu cocktail dress, photo by Rodrigo Corral Design/Tracy Morford. 163: Jason Wu french knot embroidery detail, photo by Rodrigo Corral Design/Tracy Morford. 164: Sequins on chiffon fabric used by Peter Soronen, photo by Rodrigo Corral Design/Michael Schmelling. 165: Getty Images/Mandel Ngan. 166: Illustration by Rodrigo Corral Design/Ben Wiseman. 167: White House Photo/Flickr/Public Domain. 168: Getty Images/Alex Wong. 169: AP Photo. 170: Emerald green silk chiffon fabric used by Kai Milla, photo by Rodrigo Corral Design/Tracy Morford. 171: Getty Images/Pool. 172: Illustration by Rodrigo Corral Design/Ben Wiseman. 173: Illustration by Renaldo A. Barnette. 174-175: (From left) Sonia Rykiel clear vinyl belt, photo by Rodrigo Corral Design/Tracy Morford; Rodney Choice. 176: Illustration by Rodrigo Corral Design/Ben Wiseman. 177: Getty Images/Stan Honda. 178: Getty Images/Mandel Ngan. 179: Getty Images/Win McNamee. 180: (From left) Getty Images/AFP; Jonathan Ernst/Reuters. 181: Brooks Kraft/Corbis. 182-183: Getty Images/Mandel Ngan. 184: Getty Images/Mark Wilson. 185: Getty Images/Saul Loeb. 186: (From top) J. Crew Constellation cardigan, image supplied by J. Crew – Jimmy Choo Jade pump in snakeskin, photo by Rodrigo Corral Design/Michael Schmelling. 187: (From left) Getty Images/WPA Pool; AP Photo. 188-189: Getty Images/Mandel Ngan. 190: Getty Images/John Stillwell. 191: Getty Images/Saun Curry. 192: Getty Images/WPA Pool. 193: Getty Images/Mandel Ngan. 194: (From top) Illustration by Rodrigo Corral Design/Ben Wiseman – Kevin Lamarque/Reuters/Corbis. 195: Junya Watanabe argyle cardigan, photo by Rodrigo Corral Design/Michael Schmelling. 196: Getty Images/Saul Loeb. 197: Getty Images/Saul Loeb. 198: AP Photo. 199: Fabrizio Bensch/Reuters. 200: Getty Images/Sean Gallup. 201: Getty Images/Nigel Treblin. 202: Moschino oversize bow blouse, image courtesy of Moschino. 203: Getty Images/Joe Klamar. 204-205: Getty Images/Alex Wong. 206: Getty Images/Pool. 207: Pieter Erasmus. 209: Getty Images/Jim Watson. 210: Getty Images/AFP. 211: Peter Soronen one-shoulder painted lace dress, photo by Rodrigo Corral Design/Michael Schmelling. 213: Getty Images/Win McNamee. 215: Elisabeth Moch. 216: Jean-Philippe Delhomme. 219: François Berthoud. 220: Minni Havas. 223: Mia Overgaard. 224: Virginia Johnson. 225: Carter Kustera. 226: Stephen Campbell. 228: Sirichai. 231: David Downton. 236: Getty Images/Emmanuel Dunand.